CONTENTS

Introduction

Contemporary discourse concerning the political role and application of Islam is deeply influenced by the west, as it is largely considered as either a positive or negative reaction to the western way of life. Confronted by the emerging technical and military superiority, economic achievements and apparent affluence of western society, Muslims have been forced to address the challenge of modernity and the various dimensions that accompany it. As a result, the need to review and redefine the Islamic position has become necessary, a discussion which has established two main streams of political thought amongst Muslim scholars and intellectuals.

Firstly, there are those who advocate a "liberal" interpretation of Islam and strive to demonstrate its compatibility with the underlying values of modernism and, more precisely, the western political system. Supporters of this stream see their interests and objectives in secular terms; many adopt ideologies such as nationalism, pan-Arabism, socialism and Marxism, frequently disconnecting themselves from classical Islamic political thought.

The second stream of thought, often categorised as revivalism or fundamentalism, embody an extreme reaction to the spread of western ideas throughout the Muslim world. Its followers totally reject parliamentary liberalism, amongst other western ideologies, and advocate the comprehensive adoption of the sources of divine revelation as a means to end the West's hegemony, whilst overcoming present difficulties faced by Muslim societies.

The reflexive nature of these two streams offers little beyond a positive or negative reaction to modernism and the western way of life (specifically in the political field). Followers of the former adopt a secular approach; providing an optimistic analysis of western political values, either endorsing them or assuming them as Islamic concepts. In short, this attitude provides no potential for the development or evolution of Islamic political heritage. On the other hand, despite strong aspirations to establish a pure Islamic society and government, revivalism and fundamentalism fail to provide a complete or unambiguous model for this ideal society. Many revivalists have attempted to reform the political theory of traditional Sunni jurist's (i.e. the theory of *Khilafah* or Caliphate) whilst other, more excessive versions of fundamentalism (such as the Taliban movement) present an aggressive, oppressive and backward image of the Islamic model.

Born amidst shallow and ultimately reactionary Islamic political ideologies, the theory of "Wilayat al-Faqih" constituted an entirely new direction and mode of thinking. This conception of Islamic governance, formally embodied in the constitution of the Islamic Republic of Iran, is distinguished by its close connection to Shia political doctrine and the successful amalgamation of shari'a and democracy. It composes the authority of an Islamic legal system, the political guardianship of a just and capable Mujtahid (jurist) and the democratic role of the people in the distribution of political power. Within the framework of the traditional Shi'a doctrine of Imamat, this political doctrine reconciles the authority of religion and the authority of the people.

There are many misunderstandings concerning the theory of Wilayat al-faqih, its historical background and political justification, the role of people and what separates it from other Islamic political theories (such as that of the Caliphate). The primary function of this book is to clarify these different dimensions and dispel any ambiguities surrounding this version of the Islamic state.

The wilayat al-faqih (guardianship of the scholars) is a religious model of government. It is therefore essential to discuss why we are in need of a 'religious state' and to take full account of the implications and justifications of this model in the contemporary world. Chapter one addresses the definition of a 'religious government' and explores the relationship between Islam and politics. It also assesses the principal arguments presented by various Muslim thinkers, particularly those who are opposed to the concept of an Islamic government.

Chapter two intends to clarify the doctrine of wilayat al-faqih, its historical background, what distinguishes it from other political theories, and its connection to the traditional religious authority of the Islamic jurists (Marja'a Taqleed), to whom ordinary Shia refer to and whose decrees they follow on religious affairs. All scholars and jurists accept that the Marja'a has a duty to act as vicegerent on behalf of the absent, infallible Imam. However, it is the scope of authority in this vicegerency that is contentious. The second chapter aims to expound and develop this discussion, thereby explicating the role of a jurist in the model of wilayat al-faqih.

As a political theory of state, wilayat al-faqih maintains the collective vicegerency of the faqih adil (a just or trustworthy jurist), which is the maximum scope of his authority. The third chapter will discuss the justifications of this theory and expound some of the traditional evidence provided by high-ranking jurists who support the doctrine of wilayat al-faqih.

Liberal democracy remains the prevalent political theory of our time. The final chapter of this book will deal with the dichotomy that arises between the concept of Islamic democracy, embodied in the theory of wilayat al-faqih, and the liberal interpretation of the democratic system, which exists in the majority of western countries today.

It is my hope that these four chapters will provide the reader with a comprehensive outline of Shia political thought in general, and the modern incarnation of this political thought, which is embodied in the constitution of the Islamic Republic of Iran, in particular.

At the end I would like to thank Dr: Seyyed Muhammad Marandi who encouraged me for writing the book and kindly undertook the final editing. I am grateful to Eskandar Khalili for typing and editing the manuscript of chapters three and four. Thanks also to Yasmin Merchant and Jondab who typed chapters one and two. I am grateful to all my friends and colleagues in Islamic center of England especially Shaikh Muhsen Araki and Shaikh Hamid Hadji Haidar for encouragement and offering helpful advice.

Ahmad Vaezi

Cambridge University

February 2004

Chapter One

Islam and Politics

What is a "Religious Government"?

The influence of religion upon politics is not a phenomenon that is confined solely to the Islamic world. However, it is impossible for any political theorist to ignore the role of Islam in the public lives of Muslims. Its considerable impact upon the politics of Muslim nations can be attributed to the strong inclination of the population towards it, and thus the powerful voice that it is given by them. Leaman writes:

> One of the comments which writers on Islamic Political Philosophy often make is that it is irremediably conservative. Even the so-called modernizers have in mind some sort of theocracy, a state in which religion plays a leading role.[1]

It is obvious that any legal system requires a government to adopt it and the apparatus of a state to implement and enforce it. Therefore, Islamic Law (shari'a) is also in need of a state for its sanction and application. However, the key concern then becomes whether or not all theories shaped in the history of Islamic political thought are actually seeking the establishment of an "Islamic state". The two aforementioned factors; that Islam is a vital and necessary aspect of a Muslim's culture, and that the shari'a requires

---

[1] Oliver Leaman, *A Brief Introduction to Islamic Philosophy*, Polity Press, 1999, p. 134.

political power and authority in order to be implemented, might bring one to the conclusion that all political systems in the Islamic world were historically religious governments.

Although there are obvious difficulties associated with finding a precise and agreed definition of a "religious government", it is essential to distinguish between various levels of state commitment to a specific religion. The minimal degree of dedication would be that a government did not prevent its people from undertaking their religious rituals and practices. On the other hand, a maximized relationship between religion and politics requires the total commitment and adherence of a state to the contents of a specific religion. Obviously, many varying degrees of religious authority could be supposed between these two extremes.

Official definitions of a "religious state" focus on a series of prescribed characteristics and functions embodied by this model of political system. These may be related to individual characteristics, such as a governor necessarily belonging to a specific religion or social class, similar to the governments of European states throughout the Middle Ages. One might also define a religious government according to its partial or prejudicial favour towards a particular religion. Consequently, a religious state uses its military, political and economic power to promote and strengthen the position and followers of that specific faith.

This draws our attention to a few, specific aspects of a religious government. However, it fails to adequately introduce what most contemporary Islamic political movements and doctrines have in mind when they apply the term "Islamic State", which is perhaps most effectively described as the maximum realization of a religious state.

An Islamic government's primary aim is to establish a truly Islamic society. Islam does not consider society to be merely a collection of individuals. Rather, it deems that society also consists of their social relationships and the social order in which these individuals exist. These are perhaps the most definitive factors of a society, as different societies are categorized as being just or unjust, developed or undeveloped and complex or plain, according to their social formations and their systems of rights and duties. Financial sources, social advantages and the structure of the prevailing political system, are all part of the complex web of social relationships that contribute to the makeup of society. Therefore, an Islamic society, by definition, is an ideal society in which social order is established and regulated according to underlying Islamic values, teachings and rulings.

An Islamic government is one that accepts and admits the absolute authority of Islam. It seeks to establish an Islamic social order according to the contents of Islam, implementing the shari'a, while attempting to direct its political decisions and public functions according to the aims and values of Islam.

This understanding of an Islamic state obviously faces criticism, especially from those who adopt more secular political ideologies. The following pages will assess some of the contentious aspects surrounding this theory of Islamic governance.

Rejection of Islamic Government

Opponents of Islamic governance can be divided into two major categories: The first of these are the supporters of secularism, who contend that religion must be completely separate from worldly affairs. In their eyes, the concept of a religious state is backward and outdated. They maintain that this model of political system must be confined to a time when human beings lacked the knowledge or experience to organize their social order and were in need of religion to arrange their legal, economic and cultural relationships. However, secularism is not a doctrine that merely addresses the relationship between religion and politics. Essentially, it is a radical approach to the role of religion and revelation in shaping human knowledge. Secular rationality maintains that the human intellect is capable of forming its own knowledge independent of revelation. According to this, reason in itself is self-sufficient and autonomous. Hence, mankind is capable of constructing natural and human sciences as well as philosophy, law and ethics without the aid of God or religion.

Secular thinking, therefore, leaves very little scope for religion. According to secularist thought, every instance in which the human intellect is capable of gaining knowledge exists as part of the exclusive realm of the human being, without any need for faith or revelation. Such reasoning constrains the role of religion to regulating the individual relationship between man and his creator, while isolating it from the social and political order. This is because social relationships form part of "human" affairs and not "divine" affairs; they are "extra-religious" as opposed to "intra-religious". Law, economy and political decisions as well as the formations of our social structures and systems of rights and duties are all considered as merely dealing with the relationship between man and man, not man and God. Therefore, religion in these cases must delegate everything to human reasoning and science.

This concise overview of secular thinking illustrates that the reduction of secularism to a political doctrine, which purely insists on the separation of faith from politics, is incorrect. The isolation of religion from politics is but one of the many accomplishments of secular rationality. Advocates of this view insist on the disengagement of religion, not only from politics, but also from ethics, art, law, philosophy and the sciences. Consequently, they advocate not only a secular state, but secular laws, a secular culture, a secular science and so on.

Whereas the first approach delegates a limited scope for religion, the second group of opponents have no argument with those who believe it cannot be restricted to merely having a limited, fixed or previously determined capacity. In principle, they agree that no one has the right to confine the contents and the implementation of Islam to private life, or more precisely, to the individual relationship between man and God. The central concern of the second group, however, is that although Islam embodies certain values and ideas, it is not composed of both spirituality and politics. Thus it has not specified any particular form of government and Muslims are free to support any regime they desire.

So the fundamental distinction that arises between these two groups is that, while secularists argue that religion and politics must remain separate, the second faction contend that Islam does not in any way oblige it's followers to establish it in the political realm. They attempt to demonstrate that Islam has no connection to politics by concentrating on the Holy Qur'an and early Islamic history, arguing that it is a purely spiritual doctrine, as opposed to a spiritual and political one. Secularists, on the other hand, focus on the demands of modernity, the inability of religion to conduct and organize the contemporary world, and its failure to overcome the complications presented by modernism. Therefore, it is crucial to clarify whether or not Islam compelled its followers to establish an Islamic government, and whether or not Islam is indeed capable of regulating modern society.

No credible Muslim thinker advocates the segregation of religion from worldly affairs, as the secular tradition would insist, reducing it to little more than a personal relationship between man and God. In fact, very few Islamic intellectuals appeal to secular rationality other than to insist on the separation of religion from socio-political relationships (i.e. restricting the scope of religion and extending the role of reasoning in public life). Although these thinkers do not explicitly call themselves secular, their attitudes towards the issue of Islam and politics obviously have common characteristics with those of secularists.

Having introduced the two main critical attitudes towards Islamic government, the following pages will examine the central arguments presented by adherents to these two schools of thought, beginning with the reasons provided that reject any original connection between Islam and politics.

First Argument

In his famous book "Islam and the Foundations of Government" (Al-Islam wa Usul al-Hukm) Shaykh Ali Abd al-Raziq[1] (1888-1966) sought to justify the separation of religion and political authority on the basis of religious evidences. He argued that the Prophet Muhammad (pbuh) did not intend to establish a political state in Madina and that Islam did not support the rise of any particular social system.

This assertion totally contradicted the traditional belief, which held that the Hijrah (migration to Madina in 622) marked the beginning of the Prophet's political activity and the realization of Islamic governance. Abd al-Raziq argued that the Prophet was the bearer of a religious message; he did not have a government, nor did he seek to establish a kingdom in the political sense or anything synonymous with it. Rather, his authority was sacred, derived from God so that he could deliver the divine revelation. According to Abd al-Raziq, this did not entail political leadership; it was the mandate of a Prophet and not of a Sultan.

To justify his view, Abd al-Raziq refers to several verses of the Qur'an. He believes that according to these, the Prophet Muhammad (pbuh) was only a messenger, commissioned to deliver God's revelation to the people and nothing else.

---

[1] Born in Egypt, a disciple of Shaykh Abduh, Abd al-Raziq studied at Oxford University and was a senior member of al-Azhar University, an authorative centre of Sunni learning. His short, but controversial book caused many debates in religious and political circles. Al-Azhar immediately condemned Abd al-Raziq's work; he was thrown out of the university and dismissed from his position as a religious judge.

We have sent you only to give good news and to warn.
[Chapter 17, Verse 105]

The duty of the messenger is to convey the message clearly. [Chapter 27, Verse 54]

Yet we have sent you only to give good tidings and to warn. [Chapter 25, Verse 56]

Tell him: I am only a warner. [Chapter 27, Verse 92]

Abd al-Raziq argues that if the Prophet Muhammad (pbuh) had other roles, such as that of a political leader, then the Qur'an would clearly have announced them.[2] In order to justify his position, he argues that every state requires a political structure that contains specific institutions and administrations, but that Muhammad's leadership was devoid of these necessary elements of government. In fact, according to this point of view, political authority only appeared in the Islamic community following the demise of the Messenger of God. Consequently, striving for the establishment of a government is not considered part of Islamic teachings.[3]

However, contrary to Abd al-Raziq's opinion, there is a mass of historical evidence that clearly demonstrates the Prophet's role as both a political and religious leader. In fact, many western thinkers, such as Anthony Black, agree that the Prophet's objective was not merely to establish a new identity by replacing old tribal customs. According to these

---

[2] *Islam wa Usul al-Hukm*, Cairo 1925, p. 73.
[3] *Ibid.*, pp. 62-64.

thinkers, he addressed political power as well as spiritual and cultural authority. Black writes:

> *His purpose was to construct out of tribal confederacies a new people driven by his own sense of moral mission. Judaism had preached an all-embracing (ethnic) law, While Christianity had preached spiritual (universal) brotherhood. But, neither seriously addressed the problem of military power and political authority; both had accepted life under alien, pagan rule. Muhammad preached spiritual brotherhood, plus an all-embracing law, and universal political control to be achieved.[4]*

The activities of the Prophet Muhammad following the Hijrah brought about revolutionary changes to the Arabian Peninsula. These cannot simply be interpreted as the ordinary behavior of a religious leader. Included here are concise examples of his political deeds, which 'could not have been issued without political authority.

He assembled a number of hostile tribes and forged them into a new community (ummah). This is essentially a political endeavor, which is embodied in what Montgomery Watt refers to as the "Constitution of Medina", a document that outlines the nature of the state that the Prophet was intending to establish. The charter incorporates articles concerning the rights and duties of the various tribes and social groupings that formed this new society, including

---

[4] Anthony Black, *The History of Islamic Political Thought*, Edinburgh University Press, 2001, p. 10.

their obligations regarding one another, criminal events and the rights of non-Muslim members of this community.[5]

He delegated both religious and political responsibilities to his companions. Some, such as Amr ibn Hazm, were sent to lead the prayers and teach the people about the Qur'an. Whilst others, such as Abu Musa al-Ashari and Saed ibn Aas, were dispatched as representatives to collect taxes (zakat), arbitrate disputes and punish criminals as well as to educate people about Islam. Sometimes, the Prophet would assign companions to exclusively governmental capacities, such as when he sent Abu Sufyan to gather taxes in Najran, while Amr ibn Hazm remained his religious representative in that region.[6]

The Prophet (pbuh) was a general, a diplomat and a judge. He led the army, entered into treaties and agreements with various tribes, and passed judgment in criminal cases. Issues such war, diplomatic relations and legal arbitration are all obviously included in political authority and have no connection to a specifically spiritual mandate.

Furthermore, it is unreasonable to compare the structures of a modern state and the Prophet's authority in Madina in order to determine whether he established a political state. Dr. Senhoury, for example, argues that the political order established in Madina adequately met the demands of a simple tribal community, thus there was no need to establish

---

[5] Montgomery Watt, *Islamic Political Thought*, p. 5.
[6] Tabary, *Tareekh al-Rasul wa al-Malik* (History of Messengers and Kings), volume 3, p. 318.

a complex social order when the Prophet's political system was appropriate to the requirements of his age and society.[7]

Some thinkers, such as Abid al-Jaberi, contend that because the word "dawlat" (state) was not adopted as a political term until the beginning of the Abbasid-era, the political concept of an Islamic state did not exist either. According to Al-Jaberi, the Prophet (pbuh) established an "ummah" as opposed to a state. However, although it may be true that the term dawlat was not prevalent in Arab vocabulary at the time of the Prophet, it is not the name that constitutes a state. Rather, it is the nature of the authority that establishes an Islamic government, thus it is irrelevant whether the term "state" was adopted or not.

Although Abd al-Raziq refers to several verses of the Qur'an in order to justify his opinion, which is that the Prophet (pbuh) had no role beside that of a messenger, the verses that he submits as evidence do not confine the character of the Prophet to a single attribute. A clear distinction must be made between a relative restriction and an absolute or definite restriction. The latter confines the character of a subject to one feature, whilst the former refers to a restriction in a limited scope of attributes. For example, someone supposes that x is both a writer and a poet. You correct his opinion by telling him that 'x is only a writer'. However, this does not mean that x has no other qualities apart from being a writer, because your statement restricts his character in relation to only two attributes.

---

[7] Ahmed Abd al-Razig al-Senhoury, *Fiqh ul-Khilafah wa Tataworeha* (The Jurisprudence of Caliphate and Development), Cairo, 2nd Edition, 1993, p. 82.

All the verses to which Abd al-Raziq refers fall into the first category, which is that of relative restriction. They are merely emphasizing that the Prophet has no responsibility towards those who disbelieve in his call. Certainly, the Prophet as a human being has many other qualities and duties. Therefore, emphasis upon one issue within a specific context does not nullify the possibility of other tasks or characteristics. Take, for example, following verses:

O Prophet, urge the believers to war. [Chapter 8, Verse 65]

And judge (rule) between them by what Allah has revealed, and do not follow their low desires. [Chapter 5, Verse 49]

Your Wali is none but Allah and his Messenger. [Chapter 5, Verse 55]

And We did not send a messenger except that he should be obeyed.... [Chapter 4, Verse 64]

Second Argument

Aside from those who subscribe to a view similar to that of Abd al-Raziq, other opponents of the Islamic state accept that the Prophet did, in fact, establish a political order following his migration to Madina. However, they also maintain that this does not constitute an intrinsic connection between Islam and politics. The emergence of the Prophet's authority in Madina is considered as little more than a historical event; a specific situation in which the social and political circumstances necessitated this endeavor, rather than a religious duty that was included in divine revelation.

Dr. Haery seems to adopt a similar opinion in the following passage, in which he emphasizes that the Prophet's government was formed upon the consensus of the people and then later endorsed by God. He writes:

Some previous Prophets, especially the Prophet of Islam, besides the exalted position of Prophethood had undertaken governing people and committing political affairs. We have to know that since people compelled them with no anticipate inclination, these political authorities and special circumstances forced them to accept, the Political authority cannot be taken into account as part of God's revelation.[8]

To support this point of view regarding the Prophet's authority, Haery refers to the following verse of the Qur'an:

Certainly Allah was well pleased with the believers when they swore allegiance to you under the tree. [Chapter 48, Verse 18]

He, and others who adopt a comparable opinion, insist that although God endorsed the pledge of allegiance (bay'a) given to the Prophet, His approval is not enough to make the establishment of political authority an Islamic objective.[9] However, the relationship between Islam and politics and the historical events precluding the creation of an Islamic social order are two entirely separate and distinct topics. Studying the latter requires a precise analysis of the historical, social and cultural context in that era. Whereas the former

---

[8] Mehdi Haery Yazdi, *Hekmat wa Hokumat*, London: Shadi Publication, 1995, p. 143.
[9] *Ibid.*, p. 152.

necessitates a comprehensive evaluation of the Islamic ideology to determine whether or not it encompasses a political dimension and if it has the potential to be practically applied. Thus, the correlation of historical stages and circumstances to the process of forming a government is entirely separable from our present debate, which concerns the Islamic political system. Hence, many contemporary Muslim scholars, such as Muhammad Ammareh, who is an advocate of the Islamic state, come to the following conclusion:

> *Even though the generous Qur'an did not explicitly [make it] incumbent upon Muslims to form a religious government [it obliged them] with some duties [that] would be impossible to fulfill without the establishment of an Islamic State.* [10]

Both Dr. Haery and Muhammad Ammareh maintain that the pledge of allegiance (bay'a) given by the tribal representatives of Madina to the Prophet, during the year prior to his emigration from Mecca, was the keystone of his government. However, this theory, which introduces the allegiance (bay'a) of the people as the root of the Prophet's political authority, confronts two difficulties. The first is that the contract of bay'a was a prevailing custom amongst the Arabs, which occurred for a variety of reasons; the pledge of bay'a to a political leader or tribal chief was only one of these. Accordingly, it is essential that we assess the content of these pledges used to support the arguments of Dr Haery and Muhammad Ammareh.

---

[10] Muhammad Amareh, *Al-Elmaniya wa Nehzatona*, Cairo: Dar al-Shorugh, 1986, p. 35.

The pledge mentioned in Chapter 18 of the Qur'an, known as "Bay'a rezwan", occurred at Hudaybiyah, near Mecca, in the sixth year after Hijrah. The Prophet Muhammad (pbuh) and a number of his followers were en-route to perform the pilgrimage to Mecca, when Meccan polytheists who wished to prevent them from entering the city confronted them. Under these dangerous circumstances, a number of believers pledged allegiance to the Prophet so as to reassure him that they would remain by his side and protect him from the enemies of Islam. This pledge was merely a reaffirmation of their loyalty in a difficult situation, rather than the acknowledgement of the Prophet's political authority. Furthermore, it took place five years after the establishment of the Islamic state in Madina, thus it seems strange to consider this event the original root of his government.

What is often referred to as the second pledge of allegiance known as "bay'a al-Aqabeh" also has no connection to the nomination of a ruler. Comparing it to the negotiations that took place at Saqifa, prior to the appointment of Abu Bakr, explicitly demonstrates that the pledge of al-Aqabeh was not a recognition of the Prophet's political authority. The negotiations at Saqifa were concerned with leadership following the death of Muhammad (pbuh). Hence, the bay'a at Saqifa merely served as an election, whereas the pledge of al-Aqabeh was regarding the protection and safety of the Prophet; the representatives of Madina promised to resist the polytheists and protect the Prophet as they would their own families.

The second difficulty confronted by the supporters of this argument, arises from several verses of the Holy Qur'an which delegate and approve the guardianship (wilayat) of the Prophet over the believers, with no reference to any anticipated acceptance from the people; therefore indicating that his authority is indeed divine. These verses shall be discussed in greater detail later, but for now we shall mention a few:

The Prophet has a greater claim on the faithful that they have on themselves. [Chapter 33, Verse 6]

Only Allah is your guardian (Wali) and His Apostle. [Chapter 5, Verse 55]

Third Argument

Another prevailing argument, employed by secularists to undermine the theory of a religious government focuses on the ambitions of those who support an Islamic state (i.e. the establishment of an ideal social order according to Islam and the application of the shari'a to all facets of society). Secularists, who adopt this line of reasoning, contend that a religious social order is an incompatible thesis because it is confronted by an inherent difficulty known as "the problem of accommodation". To justify this argument, they rely on two premises:

Social, economic and cultural relationships undergo constant change and development: There is a significant difference between our contemporary lifestyles and the lifestyles of previous generations in areas such as transportation, commerce, education and so on. Thus social formation is essentially variable and no one can expect a society to remain stable for a prolonged period of time.

Religion is fixed, unchanging and stable: Every religion is confined to a specific period of history; as it was founded upon the demands, circumstances and problems of a particular age. Religion is an event that happened in a determined time and place, which cannot be repeated. Consequently, the message of every religion is inflexible and has no capacity for adaptation to new situations.

Thus, a secularist would argue that because religion is a fixed and unchanging set of ideas, it is entirely incapable of accommodating changes to social relationships, which are in turn fundamentally unfixed and variable. It is entirely reasonable to admit that religion is able to form a social order, which is influenced by its conventions and ethics, but only at a time when social circumstances would permit such an influence. For example, in the time when Islam emerged, it was able to adequately meet the demands of the historical period. Thus, Islam succeeded in establishing a civilization during that era. However, it seems paradoxical to suppose that Islam is capable of effectively shaping social order under any circumstances and at any time. The core of this reasoning is that social associations and relationships are fluid and open to regular changes; no one is able to prevent these social alterations and thereby narrow them to a fixed religious form and structure. In summary, secularists assert that although shari'a has within it the competence and capability to deal with social formations similar to those existing at the time when Islam appeared, there are serious obstacles for the application of shari'a to contemporary social configurations.

Such an assessment is based on the presupposition that the conception of a religious state leaves no room for adaptation or the endorsement of social changes. Therefore, the response to this argument will discuss three significant points;

- An evaluation of this interpretation of social changes.
- Aspects of the Islamic legal system, which have been overlooked by secularists who subscribe to this opinion, that render it both dynamic and flexible.
- A clarification of what is meant by the accommodation of shari'a and the precise definition of the establishment of "Islamic social order"

Categorizing Social Alterations

No one can dispute the fluidity and variable nature of social relationships. Changes occur both radically over a short period of time, and gradually over a more prolonged period. They have numerous dimensions and affect various aspects of human life. As far as the present discussion is concerned, which is the role of religion in a well ordered society; the legal and moral dimensions are the most important ones that should be considered.

From a legal perspective, every social order and its assorted characteristics confront many questions. An efficient legal system must be able to overcome these problems and introduce a competent framework, which is able to respond to new developments that are the result of social alterations. In order to practically implement a religion that encompasses social interactions, it becomes crucial to institute a dynamic legal structure that is able to organize their juridical aspects. Because the aim of a religious state is to harmonize social order according to a religious legal system, it is therefore essential to understand the nature of the legal aspect of social alterations.

Establishing a truly Islamic society and regulating social relationships according to the Islamic ideology cannot, however, be confined to merely the legal aspects of this transformation. The moral and cultural outcomes of such a revolution are fundamental as well. An Islamic government must maximize the role of moral virtues, Islamic values and true humanity in social relationships. Advocates of the Islamic state believe that religious aims and values, stemming from moral virtues and true humanity, can lead human society towards a higher level of existence. However, the argument that denies the possibility of harmonizing social order according to Islamic laws and values usually attempts to reduce the discussion to a purely legal one, attempting to illustrate that the Islamic legal system is incapable of accommodating social changes.

Those who subscribe to this argument presuppose that social alterations result in entirely new legal problems that have no previous precedent. Hence, they argue that a religious legal system, because of its unchanging nature, cannot deal with the problems that it will be frequently confronted by.

Social changes ultimately give rise to two areas of legal discourse. The first stems from an entirely new social phenomenon, of which there is no previous record. Every legal system must define its position with regard to these. For instance, the invention of computers and the development of information technology require fresh legislation. Another example is transplantation, a new technique in medicine that requires jurists to clarify the legal aspect of this new medical ability, such as the laws regarding the exchange of natural organs between human beings. The significant factor with this first group, is that they require more than merely the application of old and current laws to new situations, rather, they require a set of absolutely new laws and up-to-date legislation.

Secondly, there are those social transformations that, despite the fact they are new, have emerged from pre-existing relationships and associations, consequently these social phenomena are new in form and not in content. Accordingly, they do not require totally new legislation or a fresh set of laws; jurists could and would categorize them according to previous legal precedents. For instance, previously there existed only a few types of companies, whereas at present there are many forms of commercial relationships. However, these are not new legal phenomena. They are distinguished from previous kinds of companies essentially in form, because they are merely new structural designs.

In short, with regard to analyzing social alterations, we must adopt the following conclusion. From a juridical perspective, social changes cannot be restricted to a single definition. Generally speaking, two streams of social transformation can be identified in this regard. On the one hand, there are the cases of completely new legal phenomena that are without previous record, while on the other there are those that possess obvious connections or similarities to previous and familiar elements within the existing legal framework, though they may have each adopted a partially, or entirely new form.

Flexibility of the Islamic Legal System

The precise criticism introduced by this argument against the concept of an "Islamic state", when we are confined to the juridical aspect, is that the Islamic legal system is incapable of coping with social transformations. Hence, because it is inflexible and unable to meet the juridical requirements of new circumstances, it cannot possibly satisfy the legal demands of human society.

In order to efficiently cope with the various societal relationships it will inevitably encounter, every legal system prerequires the existence of flexible elements in its methodology and basic foundations. Although the Islamic legal system does not contain these factors, it is essential that we realize that it has aspects that provide it with the capacity to meet and fulfill all the juridical requirements presented by the two aforementioned categories of social change.

The Islamic legal system is fully equipped to deal with the first category of social changes. Even though the historical advent of Islam occurred during a specific time and in a specific place, it is quite reasonable to extrapolate a universal, ahistorical and timeless legal framework for different aspects of social relationships. Many legal aspects of social alterations can, in fact, remain stable in spite of their formal changes. This enables Islamic law (shari'a) to form a general juridical framework for the various categories of social associations. In reference to different sections of Islamic law, there exist a selection of unchanging, absolute and general rules that, at any time and place, all Muslims are obliged to respect; they are required to harmonize their public and private relationships with these rules.   For example, in commercial affairs there are some general rules as follows:

It is incumbent upon believers to fulfill their contracts and obligations:

> *O you who believe! Fulfill the obligations.* [Chapter 5, Verse 1]

Some types of contracts and commercial agreements are prohibited because they include unlawful profit such as usury:

> *Allah has allowed trading and forbidden usury.* [Chapter 2, Verse 275]

Lawful commercial and financial contracts and covenants must fulfill some general conditions such as mutual consent without coercion and must not be subject to false methods of attaining wealth, for example, gambling:

> *O you who believe! Do not devour your property among yourselves falsely, except that it be trading by your mutual consent.* [Chapter 4, Verse 29]

These examples of obligations, prohibitions and conditions concerning one aspect of social life, even though they do not embrace all the Islamic edicts in this field, help us to confront developing models of contracts. New forms of contracts, whether they are altered versions of familiar and prevailing models or entirely original ideas without previous record, can be categorized as either lawful or unlawful according to these three principals and so on. For instance, "insurance" is an example of an entirely new contract, while purchasing books via an online bookstore is merely a new method of trading which, although formally different, is a continuation of a particular category of business. When all these new forms of contracts adopt and fulfill the framework that has been drawn by shari'a, they are considered lawful.

The other important aspect concerning the flexibility of Islamic law emerges when we take into consideration the role of covenant and promise in this context. Some verses of the Qur'an order Muslims to fulfill their promises when they enter into a covenant or agreement:

> *And fulfill the promise, surely every promise shall be questioned about.* [Chapter 17, Verse 34]

This Islamic principle enables an Islamic state to enter into international conventions, in order to make use of their advantages, even though some of these conventions are concerned with completely new forms of social relationships, such as maritime laws or laws governing airlines and international trade, of which there is no previous record in the shari'a.

The doctrine of "Ijtihad", which is the deduction of laws through reference to Islamic sources, enables a qualified Jurist (faqih) to deduce responses to both old and new questions. Every qualified faqih is free to issue new decrees with regards to subjects that have no previous record amongst other Imami jurists; thereby providing the Islamic legal system with a high degree of flexibility, which enables it to confront new situations and circumstances. This potential is reinforced in view of jurists who subscribe to a doctrine that advocates the absolute guardianship of the well-qualified faqih (wilayat-a-mutlaqih). This doctrine insists that the trustworthy jurist, who is responsible for Muslim society, has the right to legislate according to specific conditions. This subject will be discussed further in the next chapter.

Rational Management versus Juristic Management

Misconceptions surrounding the implementation of shari'a and the role of fiqh (Islamic jurisprudence) in governing a state and it's society, have given rise to two opposing groups, who erroneously come to the conclusion that the Islamic method of governance is completely incompatible with "rational management", which prevails in most modern states. This group is divided into two categories; the first of which insists that Muslims in the modern world must submit to the organization of their economic, political, social and cultural affairs through rational and technical management. In this model of regulation, the human intellect, technology and the sciences have authority, while religion remains separate from worldly affairs. Therefore all public decisions and the organizing of the fundamental structures of society are fulfilled according to the rational form of authority.

The second group, however, advocates the total authority of religion and attempts to organize social affairs by presenting absolute "juristic management". This model of management, according to them, ignores the role of humanistic sources of knowledge and instead insists that the solution to all problems must emanate solely from Islamic jurisprudence (fiqh). In other words, this school of thought endeavors to replace rationality and reference to scientific means, with religion and purely juristic solutions.

It was indicated previously that this misleading interpretation for the role of Islamic jurisprudence with regards to social management and the making of political or economic decisions, arises from a misunderstanding of the term "religious state" and "religious social order". This misconception of a religious society and state grants a foothold to the critics who wish to portray the Islamic state as backward and ignorant of the demands of the contemporary world and who depict Islam as a system that denies human knowledge, rationality and progress.

Adopting the Islamic ideology and applying its laws and aims in order to harmonize different aspects of life is one thing, and ignorance of human knowledge and rationality is another. Drawing such a sharp and distinctive line between juridical and rational management is purely fictitious, as it overlooks any possible cooperation between these two methods, while incorrectly assuming that a religious state's model of government does not overlap with that of a non-religious state's in any way, shape or form (When in fact all states are burdened with similar responsibilities). Consequently, this third model would enjoy the advantages of both methods of management and combine rationality with respect to the ultimate authority of religion. The unusual, and irrationally narrow distinction between the two models of management, fails to provide any definite reason to suppose that the integration of religious authority and rationality is either impossible or incompatible. According to the history of Islamic thought, the Shia and Mutazali schools have always believed in rationalism. They endorse the role of the human intellect as a significant source of religious knowledge alongside Islamic evidence (Qur'an and hadith).

Rationality is included with Islamic sources and reasoning is taken into account as a part of religious knowledge.

It is necessary to emphasize that organizing social relationships, in its full scope, involves many facets. These include legislation, politics and policymaking as well as industrial-economic planning, social services and education. It is incorrect to suppose that, under an Islamic government, these functions and tasks would be undertaken exclusively by jurists and that all types of social, economic and cultural difficulties would be resolvable by jurisprudence. In fact, the fundamental distinction between an Islamic state and a secular one should be based on the acceptance or denial of the authority of Islam in social affairs, rather than the denial of rationality and scientific knowledge. An Islamic authority would address the needs of a society according to the criteria laid down by Islam; the extent to which jurisprudence and shari'a influence this depends on the depth to which Islam has defined the subject matter. For instance, the role of shari'a is greater in legislation than in policy making or international politics. The various elements of an Islamic government must harmonize and adapt their functions, policies and decisions to the contents of Islam, though they are able to employ their reasoning and scientific knowledge wherever it is required.

In conclusion, the allegation that Islam is somehow unable to cope with social progress or changes to various aspects of human existence is false. Islam cannot be confined to a specific time or set of circumstances, as it has within it the capacity to guide humanity towards happiness at all times. However, Islam's ability to adapt to the demands of various social formations and situations should not be taken to mean that Islam has a passive attitude towards alternative lifestyles. It is illogical to assume that every kind of cultural, social or economic relationship can be universally endorsed by Islam, for it has timeless rules, values and objectives that disagree with certain types of associations and lifestyles. This approach is not the product of essential links to a specific model of social formation or a particular social order. Rather, it is an active and dynamic attitude that emerges from a set of unchanging rules and principals that are not restricted to a specific age or generation.

Objectives of an Islamic State

Ideological aims and functions are an essential part of any political system, as they serve to distinguish and separate it from alternative doctrines. Objectives such as creating a welfare state and extending education or promoting prosperity and defending a nation's borders are not specific to any one model of political system. In fact, almost all political theories commonly emphasize upon these targets. Therefore, it is necessary that we define the unique objectives of a religious government and discuss how they set it apart from other political systems.

Implementation of the Shari'a

The application of Islamic laws and rulings is a fundamental aspect of the religious state. A government that neglects the shari'a cannot be considered a legitimate Islamic authority; as such a notion is paradoxical and ultimately self-contradicting. The Holy Qur'an obliges the believers to implement, protect and respect Islamic laws in all spheres of their public and private lives. For example, take the following verses:

And we have revealed to you the Book with the Truth, verifying what is before it of the book and a guardian over it, therefore, judge between them by what Allah revealed. [Chapter 5, Verse 48]

And whoever does not judge by what Allah has revealed, they are the unbelievers. [Chapter 5, Verse 44]

Allah raised prophets as bearers of good news and warners, and He revealed with them the book with truth, that it might judge between people in that in which they differed. [Chapter 2, Verses 2 & 3]

These are the limits of Allah, so do no exceed them, and whoever exceeds the limits of Allah, these it is that are the unjust. [Chapter 2, Verse 229]

And if you differ in anything amongst yourselves, refer it to Allah and His messenger. [Chapter 4, Verse 59]

For the government and citizens of the Islamic state to fulfill this duty, it becomes essential for the state's laws to be consistent with the shari'a and it's ruling system to be founded upon the principals of Islamic jurisprudence (fiqh). As pointed out, many modern Muslim intellectuals have criticized this jurisprudential conception, insisting that shari'a must be separated from governance, public affairs and the shaping of the system of human rights and duties that regulate society. They maintain that these should be governed according to human sciences, rationality and an extra-religious conception of human rights, rather than through Islamic jurisprudence. This ultimately secular approach belittles the importance of the shari'a and its practical necessity in an Islamic state. This approach shall be further assessed in the final chapter when considering the arguments of those who seek to reconcile Islam with liberal democracy.

To Enjoin the Good and Forbid the Evil

Islam has made it incumbent upon believing men and women to establish a healthy society, which is purified of corruption and wrongdoing and conducts itself correctly and avoids injustice. This duty is embodied in the principal of "al-amr' bi'l maruf' wal-nahi an al-munkar" (Enjoining the good and forbidding the evil) that is mentioned in the following verses of the Qur'an:

> And from among you there should be a party who invite to good and enjoin what is right and forbid the wrong and these it is that shall be successful. [Chapter 3, Verse 104]

> And (as for) the believing men and the believing women, they are guardians of each other; they enjoin good and forbid evil. [Chapter 9, Verse 71]

Calling people to what is right and preventing injustice is the joint responsibility of the state and its citizens. An Islamic government cannot remain neutral concerning the moral-religious conditions of society. Also, as well as being accountable for affairs such as security, welfare and social order, the government is also charged with maintaining human virtues, common good, morality and religious commitment. Unlike most contemporary political theories, especially those formed upon the traditions of liberalism,

Islam does not support the concept of a 'limited state'. According to this liberal approach, the authority of a government is limited by the scope and framework defined by liberalism and it's interpretation of human rights and social justice, which are connected to the underlying values of liberal doctrine. Consequently, the government is rendered unable to adopt a partial position with regards to morality, religion or ethics. Whether someone is moral or immoral, religious or irreligious, these are regarded as individual matters that the individual is able to choose as he pleases. Only if the individual break the law or violates the rights of others is the liberal government allowed to interfere in their affairs.

However, it must be pointed out that the duty of a religious government, regarding the moral-religious position of society, does not allow Muslim rulers or citizens to impose Islamic beliefs and values upon others. Religious tolerance is a significant characteristic of the Islamic ideology; a fact to which history testifies. For example, the Jews and Christians of the Spanish Peninsula enjoyed the same rights, security and prosperity afforded to all citizens of the Islamic state, as did many other ethnic and religious minorities throughout the domain of Islam at that time.

The nature of a religious government's responsibility regarding the moral condition of society is concerned primarily with decision-making, legislation and government policy. An Islamic state is obliged to maximize the opportunities to promote spirituality, moral values and individual virtues, while providing the people with a stable environment in which to attain a comfortable, safe and fruitful existence. Essentially, its role is to maintain a healthy social atmosphere. People are free to adopt their own beliefs and opinions, but in public they must respect and abide by Islamic laws. For instance, it is not the duty of an Islamic government to monitor the private lives of it's people to discover whether or not they drink alcohol, but no one is allowed to publicly consume the substance, as this would damage the social environment, and it is the responsibility of an Islamic authority to protect society from corruption and immorality.

From the Islamic view the problem of happiness and wickedness eventually rests on the choice made by the individual. Almighty God says:

Surely we have shown him the way; he may be thankful or unthankful. [Chapter 76, Verse 3]

That is because those who disbelieve follow falsehood, and those who believe follow the truth from their Lord. [Chapter 47, Verse 3]

Therefore an individual is allowed to adopt his or her personal wishes and ideas in private, but these cannot be allowed to infringe upon the moral health and stability of society. Nothing must prevent the government and believers from striving to create desirable social circumstances, or promoting Islamic values in order to remove the obstacles in the path of a truly correct and fulfilling lifestyle.

Modern political doctrines tend to emphasize human rights, rather than human goods. For them, it would be more desirable and practical if we concentrated on defining the mutual duties of the rulers and the ruled according to the rights of human beings. This is because other concepts such as happiness, virtue and social good are often ambiguous, subjective and controversial. For example, there is a strong tradition in political thought that amongst the members of any polity there is a common good and the function of the government is to determine and actualize this. However, adversaries argue that there are a number of significant difficulties regarding the idea of a "common good". Modernist political thinkers usually ask "what is a common good? and how are we to know what it is?" Robert Dahl says:

> *Every attempt I have seen to prescribe the common good is either too limited to be generally accepted or too general to be very relevant and helpful.* [11]

The Islamic doctrine approaches this problem of "common good" by extending it beyond the boundaries of a community. Not only do the members of a community have a common good but also all human beings have a common good. Islam believes that human beings share common inclinations and needs, which they are able to fulfill correctly through their own actions with the aid of a desirable, just and true Islamic government.

To Protect True Freedom of Human Beings

Liberty is arguably one of the most important underlying values upon which contemporary western political thought is founded. Although there are contending analyses regarding the nature of freedom amongst western thinkers, liberals

---

[11] Robert Dahl, *Democracy and its Critics*, Yale University Press, 1989, p. 283

traditionally recognize individual freedom as the most fundamental human value and they define and evaluate all other values according to their relationship with it.[12] Because most people, especially in the west, adopt a liberal conception of liberty, they often have reservations about whether a truly religious government can promote the freedom of its subjects. At a glance, it may seem strange to suppose that Islam, with its binding nature and limitations, could act as an effective safeguard of human freedom. But before proceeding with this discussion, it is appropriate to explore and assess the liberal theory of freedom.

Also known as the negative view of liberty, the liberal conception of freedom has come to be understood as the absence of coercion. This definition of freedom emanates from the works of thinkers such as Hobbes and Bentham, who envisaged it merely as the absence of external, physical or legal impediments. However, this theory fails to acknowledge less immediate or obvious obstacles to freedom, such as lack of awareness, false consciousness, repression or other inner factors of this kind. In fact, it insists that to speak of such inner factors as relevant to the issue of freedom, is to abuse words. The only clear meaning that can be given to this perception of freedom is the absence of external obstacles.[13]

---

[12] For instance Immanuel Kant in 'Theory and practice' defines justice as 'the restriction of each individual's freedom so that it harmonizes with the freedom of everyone else'. For him justice is more than a condition in which external freedom is guaranteed to all, it is a condition of maximum liberty for all.
Allen Rosen, *Kant's Theory of Justice*, Cornell University Press, 1993, pp. 9-11.
[13] Charles Taylor, "What's Wrong with Negative Liberty?" in *Contemporary Political Philosophy*, Robert E. Goodin (ed), Blackwell, 1997, p. 418.

Alternatively, the positive view of liberty asserts that freedom involves the realization of some specific capacities, abilities and powers. And it implies that if these are not realized, then the individual is not truly free, even if he or she is not subject to external coercion. Whereas negative freedom is best described as 'freedom from' (compulsion), positive freedom can be termed as 'freedom to', meaning that an individual must be free to realize his capabilities. Therefore, it is necessary for positive freedom to adopt a theory concerning human nature and a set of ideas about human needs and abilities.[14]

Taylor maintains that the positive perception of freedom concerns the exercising of control of ones life:

> Doctrines of positive freedom are concerned with a view of freedom which involves essentially the exercising of control over one's lives; one is free only to the extent that one has effectively determined oneself and the shape of ones life. The concept of freedom here is an exercise-concept.[15]

According to the Islamic conception of human nature, we are subject to various desires and capacities. Those who follow merely their natural instincts will remain in the prison of their low desires, unable to realize their potential. But those who exercise control over themselves and strive for self-purification, rather than merely obeying their impulses, are truly free. The Qur'an says:

---

[14] Rymond Plant, *Modern Political Thought*, Blackwell, 1991, p. 222-3.
[15] Charles Taylor, *Contemporary Political Philosophy*, Blackwell, 1997, p. 419.

Have you considered the one who takes his low desires as his Master; Allah has made him err having knowledge and has set a seal upon his ear, his heart and placed a covering upon his eyes. Who can then guide him after Allah? Will you not then be mindful? [Chapter 45, Verse 23]

Then know that they only follow their low desires, and who is more erring than he who follows his low desires without any guidance from Allah? Surely Allah does not guide the unjust people. [Chapter 28, Verse 50]

From this perspective, namely the positive interpretation of freedom, Islam should be recognized as a perfect form of guidance from Allah and a divine means to achieve true human freedom. The Qur'an says:

Those who follow the Apostle Prophet, the ummi, whom they find written down with them in the Taurat [Torah] and the Injeel [Gospel], (who) enjoins them good and forbids them evil, and makes things lawful to them the good things and makes unlawful to them impure things, and removes from their burden and the shackles which were upon them, so (as for) those who believe in him and honor him and help him, and follows the light which has been sent down with him, there is it that are the successful. [Chapter 7, Verse 157]

This verse among many others like it, state that the revelation received by the Prophet was sent as guidance to all mankind. That Islam is able to free human beings from the shackles placed upon them by their low desires, to raise them from a state of ignorance (concerning God and the hereafter) and to elevate them to a position of enlightenment and progress. By submitting oneself to the divine revelation and teachings of the Prophet, the individual is making an obvious commitment to worship and obey God, to control oneself and to accept certain limitations. In other words, Islam is a religion; a way of life that encompasses both spiritual and worldly aspects, thus obliging its followers to follow a specific lifestyle. This disagrees with the liberal 'negative' conception of human liberty, because it establishes boundaries and limitations upon freewill. But according to the Islamic point of view, these limitations help them to attain true freedom embodied in spiritual life and nearness to Allah.

In conclusion, one of the key objectives of an Islamic state is to prepare a desirable social condition, so that people are able to realize their full capacities, and thus free themselves from burdens. This self-realization means that people can promote their individual virtues and prepare themselves for the ultimate salvation.

Establishing a just society and respecting human equality Justice (Adl) and Equality (Qest) are two of the most important aspects of the Islamic ideology. There are many verses of the Qur'an that oblige the believers to treat people equally and to deal with them justly.

Certainly we sent our apostles with clear arguments, and sent down with them the book and the balance that men may conduct themselves with equity. [Chapter 57, Verse 25]

Surely Allah commands you to make over trusts to their owners and that when you judge rule between people you judge with justice. [Chapter 4, Verse 58]

O you who believe, be maintainers of justice, bearers of witness of Allah's sake, though it may be against your own-selves or your parents or near relatives, if he be rich or poor, Allah is nearer to them in compassion; therefore, do not follow low desires, lest you deviate; and if your swerve or turn aside, then surely Allah is aware of what you do. [Chapter 4, Verse 135]

These concepts of justice and equality encompass many different aspects of individual and public affairs. With specific regard to politics, they require the government to ensure that all people are granted an equal entitlement to citizenship, protection, the rights granted by Islam, and the benefits that accompany it, regardless of their ethnicity, beliefs or talents.

However, the establishment of a society upon justice and equality does not require 'legal equality'. Meaning that it does not need to adopt a legal system that endorses universal and indiscriminate rights and duties for all members of that society. In fact, in its most precise definition, legal equality is clearly impractical. All contemporary legal systems adopt legal inequalities within their structures of rights and duties. In politics for example, no democratic state allows children to vote, while in economics the salary of a qualified expert is greater than that of a labourer. Equally so, the Islamic legal system, which was revealed as divine law, includes legal inequalities. These arise in cases such as that of inheritance, where the share of a woman is less than that of a man. Therefore, social justice and fair governance cannot be defined as merely overlooking all categories of inequality. Instead, Islamic social justice is realized by the correct and complete implementation of the Islamic laws (shari'a) and values without exception.

Thus an Islamic state is distinguished by the objectives stated above, which have been laid down by the Qur'an and Islamic traditions. Other objectives include the eradication of tyranny, the promotion of tolerance and peaceful co-existence with non-Muslims in Islamic territory, the dissemination of knowledge amongst the people and the creation of a welfare society in order to decrease the economic divide between the rich and the poor. Finally, it is also essential that the Islamic government should be led by a just and well-qualified leader, so that it may realize it's fundamental aims. This is emphasized in the following tradition of Imam Rida (peace be upon him):

Some of the reasons behind appointments of lawful amirs (holders of authority) by God and making their obedience obligatory are as follows: Firstly, people would feel duty bound to follow certain rulers that would rescue them from corruption. It is not possible to follow such rulers unless power is entrusted on a trustee ruler. Secondly, prosperity of nations depends on the existence of rulers who try to solve their temporal and spiritual problems. God, the Wise, never leaves His creatures without a guide. The third reason is that, in the absence of a right leader and guide, the religious   commandments   and   orders   would · be   ruined.[16]

Spheres of Islamic Political Thought

At present, there is a significantly broad scope for political debates. Many scholars and intellectuals examine various spheres of political thought such as political philosophy, political ideology, political science and political systems. Thinkers who explore the relationship between Islam and politics are usually interested by what sort of political knowledge Islam provides, whether or not Islam supports political philosophy or advocates a specific political ideology and whether or not Islamic sources support a particular form of political system.

Historically, Islamic political thought has been concerned with leadership; the means of appointing a political authority and the qualities that a ruler must possess. One might suppose that Islam has restricted the discussion ·to a particular area of debate, and that it therefore overlooks many serious political concerns. However, it is necessary for us to distinguish between the political heritage of Muslim thinkers and what is provided by the contents of Islam. The political heritage of Muslims is embodied in the works of a selection of prominent Shia and Sunni jurists, philosophers and theologians, whose disciplines can be placed into four major categories: "political theology", "political philosophy", "political jurisprudence" and "political ethics". It is essential that we briefly review these aspects of Islamic

---

[16] Muhammad ibn Ali ibn Babwayh (al-shaykh al-Saduq), *Ellal al-Shariah*, Qom: Maktiba Davari, p. 253.

political thought in order to clarify the perspective and nature of the discussions in the following chapters.

i) Political Theology

The nature of Islamic political debates has been deeply influenced by a long history of theological (kalam) disagreement between Shia and Sunni scholars. Shia political thought, the original and oldest Islamic political theory, is essentially theological because its primary concern is leadership; the characteristics of the rightful leader and the correct method of identifying and appointing him. The Shia school of thought does not restrict these issues to a solely political or juridical (fiqh) discussion, rather they are considered a fundamental component of the Islamic ideology. Imamate is the focal point of this aspect of political thought and many books have been written by an assortment of thinkers from different sects on this topic.

ii) Political Philosophy

Political philosophy refers to a set of political consequences that are inferred from fundamental metaphysical-moral issues. The political writings of Al-Farabi are a typical example of Islamic achievements in this field. By definition, political philosophy should remain independent of any particular religious system or set of beliefs, as it is based upon metaphysical and rational foundations. However, Islamic political philosophers have formed deeply rational grounds for many Islamic doctrines before applying these as religious-philosophical premises in their political philosophy.

To deny the validity of Islamic political philosophy is to ignore the philosophical and ideological aspects of political issues. Many philosophical problems in politics have a close relationship with religion. And there are many Islamic teachings that offer, either directly or indirectly, suitable answers to some essential questions in political philosophy.

iii) Political Ethics

Political ethics (or the morals of politics) refers to a series of writings from Muslim scholars, who have attempted to advise and guide rulers to a successful and just method of government. These prescriptions were usually accompanied by stories of previous kings and rulers. They were collections of Islamic teachings, Greek philosophy and some elements of Persian literature. Examples of these include "Siyasat Nameh" (Book of Government) of Nidham al-Mulk (1020-1092), and "Nasihat al-Mulk" (Advice to King) of Ghazzali (1058-1111).

iv) Political Jurisprudence

Muslim jurists (fuqaha) adopted the method of political jurisprudence (or "fiqh ul-siyasi") to explicate and define the Islamic political system and juridical aspects of political affairs. They discussed the duties of rulers over their subjects, the means for appointing and the grounds for dismissing of political leaders, the personal qualities that an Imam or Deputy (caliph) should possess, and the relationship between different elements of the government to one another. Political jurisprudence overlaps political theology in several areas, such as the discussion concerning leadership. However, political jurisprudence is distinguished by its methodology and the large scope of its subject matter.

"Al-ahkam as-sultaniyya", written by the jurist Al-Mawardi between 1045 and 1058, is a good example of this facet of Islamic political heritage.

The assumption that Islam has a political ideology implies that it is impossible for one of these disciplines of political thought to illuminate its dimensions in isolation from the others. Ideology, as a political term, refers to a collection of ideas and instructions that are capable of directing political action. Every political ideology includes ultimate aims and offers a particular form of political regime that emphasizes upon specific norms, values and rights in order to draw a framework for all political affairs. In summary, a political ideology is a set of ideas that is considered as a decisive solution for the political aspects of human life. It attempts to adjust and arrange political relationships according to determined ideas and directives. Every political ideology ultimately relies upon political philosophy, because it must express its position according to fundamental political-philosophical issues, namely questions concerning human nature, the concept of justice, freedom and it's limitation and the relationship between liberty and equality and so on.

From this brief exploration of political ideology, it becomes clear how extensive the dimensions of a comprehensive political theory might be. Thus, any explanation of Islamic political ideology must develop all four aspects of Islamic political heritage; especially regarding political philosophy and jurisprudence.

However, it is not the intention of this book to explicate the entire Islamic political system, including the wide disputes and disagreements amongst the various Islamic sects and movements. The focus of the following pages will be on Imami political theory, which is known as the doctrine of Imamate in the age of the present, infallible Imam, and as "wilayat al-faqih" in the age of the absent Imam. Although, in order to keep this book concise, the political ideology shall not be discussed in great depth, the most important aspects of it will be clarified. The content and debate of the next chapters will be a composition of theological, philosophical and mostly Islamic juridical (fiqh) discussions.

Chapter Two

What is Wilayat al-Faqih?

The doctrine of wilayat al-faqih forms the central axis of contemporary Shia political thought. It advocates a guardianship-based political system, which relies upon a just and capable jurist (faqih) to assume the leadership of the government in the absence of an infallible Imam. However, although the guardianship of a high-ranking religious scholar is universally accepted amongst all Shia theories of governance, any disagreement is focused on the details such as the role of the jurist and the scope of his authority.

Because the theory of wilayat al-faqih has emerged from Imamate - which constitutes a cornerstone of Shi'ism – it is necessary to understand this political doctrine within the context of this concept of leadership. By comparing it to the tradition political theory of Sunni jurists – the doctrine of caliphate – and characterizing it's major features, we will be able to better understand and appreciate the doctrine of wilayat al-faqih.

In order to overcome the ambiguities surrounding the relationship between wilayat al-faqih and the position of an Islamic jurist as a source of guidance and imitation (Marja'a e-taqleed), it is necessary to discuss the various dimensions of guardianship in the absence of the infallible Imam. Also in order to respond to those who suppose that this doctrine is an entirely new thesis, which has only recently appeared in Shia jurisprudence, and argue that it opposes the traditional position of scholars and jurists, it is vital to briefly explain the historical background of wilayat al-faqih amongst the Imami Shia School of Islamic thought.

The Concept of Imamate

The political status of the Imams is an essential component of Imami Shi'ism. They are considered to be the true successors of the most noble Prophet Muhammad (pbuh), and those who subscribe to this Islamic perspective believe that any successor must be appointed by Allah, through his Prophet. However, there are those who attempt to reduce Imamism to a merely political attitude, a party that supports Imam Ali (pbuh) and his family as the sole legitimate successor to the Holy Prophet. Hence many Sunni scholars define Shi'ism as follows:

> *Shia are those who especially follow Ali and maintain his leadership and succession of the Prophet by his appointment (nass) and testament openly (publicly) or privately, and also believe that Ali's authority (awla) never goes out of his descendants.*[1]

But the political authority of the Imams does not imply that their role and status are restricted to governance or leadership. For their followers, the Imams represent the highest level of piety and they embody the same qualities as exemplified by the most noble Messenger of God. As Anthony Black describes them:

---

[1] Abdul-Karim Shahrestany, *Al-Melal wal-Nehal*, Cairo, 1956, volume 1, p. 131.

The twelve Imams themselves, and above all the present twelfth or hidden Imam, were held to be necessary to the constitution of the Universe and of true religion. The Imam is God's proof (Hujjah: guarantee), he is the pillar of the Universe, the 'gate' through whom God is approached. Knowledge of revelation depends upon him.[2]

Some of the qualities attributed to the Imams, such as "proof of God" (Hujjah) and "the guardian" (Wali), which are discussed later, refer to their great authority and are essential to understanding Shia political thought. Ayatollah Khomeini described "proof of God" as follows:

A 'proof of God' is one whom God has designated to conduct affairs, all his deeds, actions, and sayings constitute a proof for the Muslims. If someone commits an offence, will be made to the 'proof' for adducing evidence and formulating the charge. If the 'proof' commands you to perform a certain act, to implement the penal provisions of the law in a certain way, or to spend the income derived from booty, zakat, and sadaqa in a certain manner and if you fail to obey him in any of these respects, then God Almighty will advance a 'proof' against you on the day of Judgment.[3]

The Imams are considered to be the successors of the Prophet (pbuh) and the rightful recipients of his authority. This is not because they are from his family; rather, it is

---

[2] Antony Black, *The History of Islamic Political Thought*, p. 41.
[3] Ruhollah Khomeini, *Islam and Revolution*, Hamid Algar (tr), Berkeley: Mizan Press, 1981, p. 86.

because they are pious, obedient to Allah and embody characteristics that are pre-required for this level of religious-political leadership. Equally so, they are not appointed by any popular consensus; Imamate is instituted by divine installation (nasb); only Allah truly knows who possesses the qualities required to fulfill this duty, therefore only He is capable of appointing them. Shia considers Imamate, like Prophethood, to be a fundamental belief, and obedience to the authority of their Imam a religious obligation. Other than receiving divine revelation, which is specifically for the prophets, the Imams have all the qualities, duties and authority of the Prophet (pbuh). Political and religious guidance emanate from them and they are guardians over the believers. This is a manifestation of Allah's guardianship over human beings.

In addition to this, the concept of guardianship is another crucial element of Shia political doctrine.

Imam as "Wali"

In many verses of the Qur'an, God introduces himself as "Guardian of the Believers" (Wali ul-Mumineen):

Allah is the Guardian of the believers. [Chapter 3, Verse 68]

Allah is the Guardian of those who believe. [Chapter 2, Verse 257]

Allah suffices as a Guardian. [Chapter 4, Verse 45]

And according to several verses of the Qur'an, this guardianship has been delegated to the Prophet, so his authority is rooted in the aforementioned Divine authority:

Only Allah is your Guardian (Wali) and His Apostle. [Chapter 5, Verse 55]

The Prophet has a greater claim on the faithful than they have on themselves. [Chapter 33, Verse 6]

Verses such as these illustrate that the authority and guardianship of the Prophet was originally established and legitimized by Allah's appointment. Following this interpretation, the followers of the Imams provide a large number of traditions and historical evidence that confirm the delegation of the Imams, by Allah, through the Prophet (the doctrine of appointment) as "guardians of the believers" (Wali ul-Mumineen). Although the consequences of this doctrine will be considered over the following pages, at this point it would be helpful to discuss the meaning of the terms "Wali" and "Wilayat" and their usage, especially with regards to jurisprudence (fiqh).

Arabic lexicographers have mentioned several meanings for the word "Wali", such as:

1. Friend
2. Supporter
3. Devoted
4. Protector.

There are a series of words derived from the root of "Wali", for instance "Wilayat", "Mawla" and "Mawala Alayh". By considering the context to which these are applied, it becomes apparent that they apply to the situation that someone's affairs have been taken charge of by someone else. Therefore, whoever takes charge of these affairs is the latter's Wali, and consequently it is often applied to governance as well.[4]

When the term "Wilayat" is attributed to the Imams, it carries the implications of "mastership", "sovereignty" and "lordship". This is to indicate the authority of the Imam over the believers, who are subject to his guardianship. Imami theologians refer to the Qur'an (especially Chapter 5, Verse 55) and prophetic traditions to support the exclusive authority (wilayat) of the Imams.

The absolute authority and guardianship of Allah (wilayat al-mutlaqih) forms a central pillar of Imami political thought, which maintains that whoever wishes to exercise this authority must be appointed by Him. It is this idea that distinguishes Imamism from all other political theories and even other sects of Shi'ism; because although all schools of Shia thought agree that the Imam is subject to divine appointment through the Prophet, only Imamism tries to sustain this approach under circumstances when the infallible Imam is absent. In this doctrine, it is Allah alone who holds the absolute authority and He has explicitly appointed the Prophet and a number of believers (his family,

---

[4] Lewis writes:

'vali and vilayat are the Turkish pronunciation of the active participle and verbal noun of the Arabic root w-l-y, 'to be near' and hence 'to take charge of'; they mean respectively, governor, and governorship or province'.

Bernard Lewis, *The Political Language of Islam*, The University of Chicago Press, 1988, no. 22, p. 123.

i.e. the Ahlul-Bayt) as guardians (Wali), who are entrusted with authority over the Muslims.

> *Only God is your Wali and His Apostle and those who believe. Who perform prayer and pay alms while they bow.* [Al-Qur'an, Chapter 5, Verse 55]

The last phrase, "those who believe", according to Shia commentators refers to the Imams, whose wilayat was instituted through their appointment by the Prophet.[5]

However, what truly distinguishes the Imami political doctrine from all other forms of Shia political thought emerges from the Imami concept of leadership during the period of greater occultation; in which the Twelfth Imam is absent. The Imami creed adopts a system of vicegerency, whereby the authority (wilayat) is entrusted to the just and capable scholar (faqih e-adil), who acts as a deputy to the absent Imam. Thus, the guardianship of a jurist is legitimized and his authority is related to the original and absolute authority of Allah. A clear distinction must be drawn, however, between the authority of Imamate and the guardianship of the scholars. The Imams, whose authority is established upon their explicit designation by the Prophet, delegate and entrust a degree of their authority to those who possess specific qualities (such as justice and jurisprudence in the case of the fuqaha). So whereas the Imams were specifically appointed as guardians of legitimate authority, the jurists (fuqaha) are not explicitly selected by name, but

---

[5] For more information about the verse and some debates that have arisen by the verse among Shi'a and Sunni scholars refer to:
Abdul Husayn Sharafud-Din, *Al-Muraja'at*, Yasin T. al-Jibouri (tr), World Ahlul Bayt Islamic League (WABIL), pp. 173-180.

rather implicitly chosen as those who possess the correct qualities for leadership.

The scope of a jurist 's authority and the realm of his vicegerency constitute the most essential, while simultaneously controversial element of Imami political thought. However, before entering this crucial debate, it is important to distinguish Imami political doctrine from the political system advocated by the traditional Sunni Jurists, which is the doctrine of Caliphate.

The Theory of Caliphate

Despite the common disagreement amongst their schools of jurisprudence, Sunni jurists have traditionally advocated a specific theory of state known as Caliphate; a doctrine that, both as a political theory and significant historic reality, dominated the Islamic community for a considerable amount of time. In the interests of the present discussion, it is necessary to differentiate between the theory of Caliphate and the doctrine of Imamism.

Caliph essentially means successor, or one who assumes a position previously held by another. However, this word is not confined to the context of political authority, so a caliph may not simply be the successor of a previous governor, but also someone who is definitely appointed as a deputy and entrusted with authority by the person who appoints him, somewhat synonymous with 'deputy' or 'vicegerent'.[6]

Historically, the early Muslims are said to have applied the title of Khalifa to the first four rulers after the Prophet

---

[6] Montgomery Watt, *Islamic Political Thought*, pp. 32-33.

(Pbuh). In it's most basic meaning, the Khalifa is one who exercises governance in place of the Prophet. Abu-Bakr was once approached by a man, who asked him "Are you the deputy of the messenger of Allah?" to which Abu-Bakr replied, "No." The man asked, "So who are you"? Abu-Bakr answered, "I am the successor of the Prophet."[7] Montgomery Watt writes:

> *Since Abu-Bakr was not appointed by the Prophet except to deputize for him in leading the public prayers, the phrase "Khalifa of the messenger of God" cannot have meant 'deputy'. The primary meaning must have been merely 'successor'.[8]*

Although many rulers of the Ummayid dynasty attempted to attach a divine status to the title of successor (Caliph), Sunni Jurists generally consider the Caliph to be a legitimate ruler who governs and directs the state and it's society. His appointment is dependant upon specific qualities that the ruler must possess, however there is no universal agreement as to what these characteristics must be.

This source of disagreement initiated the first political divergence amongst the Muslims, which precipitated, sustained and continues to sustain a theological debate with focuses on legitimate leadership following the death of the Prophet (pbuh). However, the theory of Caliphate was not enshrined until the reign of the Abbasids, when it was devised and formulated by Sunni Jurists. Black writes:

---

[7] Ibn Assir, *Al-Nehaya*, Volume 1, p. 315.
[8] Montgomery Watt, *Islamic Political Thought*, p. 33.

An articulate community, traditionalist political theory was finally formulated in the first half of the eleventh century. Its doctrine of the vicegerency met the requirements of the emerging religious community by radically scaling down expectations placed on the deputy, while retaining the legitimacy of the 'Abbasids as leaders of the Muslims. The first four rightly guided (Rashidun) deputies were now placed in a special category. The immediate motive was to safeguard the 'Abbasids Caliphate against alternatives, Shia Imamism or Isma'ilism.[9]

The first, and most significant Sunni Jurist who attempted to systemize the doctrine of Caliphate within an Islamic juridical framework was Abu'l Hasan Al-Mawardi (Basra 979 – Baghdad 1058). He was a Shafi'i judge in Nishapur, and later became the chief Justice of Baghdad. In his famous book "al-ahkam as-sultaniyya" (the laws of governance), al-Mawardi attempts to legitimize the authority of the Abbasid government, while striving to justify the use of coercion as an implement of governance. He argued that a caliph is divinely entrusted with authority in political, as well as religious affairs.[10]

He writes:

God ...ordained for the people a leader through whom he provided for the vicegerency of the Prophet and through whom he protected the religious association; and he entrusted government to him, so that the management of affairs should proceed (on the basis of) right religion...The leadership became the

---

[9] Antony Black, *The History of Islamic Political Thought*, p. 84.
[10] *Ibid.*, p. 87.

principle upon which the bases of the religious association were established, by which the well-being of the people was regulated.[11]

When examining this perspective, it is important to realize that the traditional advocates of Caliphate are often inspired and influenced by the Ash'ari School of Islamic thought. This particular doctrine emphasizes divine predestination (taqdir) and the will of God as a unique agent in the world. Naturally, the fundamental principle of this doctrine brings them to the conclusion that one person, solely by the will of Allah, will succeed to gain political authority.

Abu'l-Fadl Bayhaqi (995-1077) writes:

Know that the Lord most high has given one power to the Prophets and another power to Kings, and he has made it incumbent upon the people of the earth that they should submit themselves to the two powers and should acknowledge the true way laid down by God.[12]

Al-Ghazzali in his Advice to kings says:

God has singled out two groups of men and given them preference over others: one group is the Prophets and the other is kings. Prophets he sends to His servants to lead them to Him and Kings to restrain them from (aggression against) each other.[13]

---

[11] The paragraph is translated in:
Ann K. S Lambton, *State and Government in Medieval Islam*, Oxford University Press, 1981, p. 85.
[12] Bernard Lewis, *The Political Language of Islam*, p. 134.
[13] Antony Black, *The History of Islamic Political Thought*, p. 94.

This outlook, which assumes that the authority of a Caliph includes everything and that they are naturally predestined according to the eternal will of God, is naturally compatible with the opinion currently adopted by contemporary Sunni Jurists, who argue that Allah and the Prophet did not appoint a particular person or persons as rulers over the Muslims. After all, the logical consequence of this concept of predestination and unique divine agency is that it doesn't matter who governs or how he obtains authority, for in any case and circumstance it would be subject to the will of God. This is the first distinction between Shi'a political thought and the doctrine of Caliphate. For Imamites the legitimate authority must be designated - directly or indirectly - by God.

The second distinction that must be made, however, concerns the method of appointing a Caliph. Imami political theory maintains that there is only one legitimate means to designate authority; divine installation. Even the guardianship of just and capable jurists (faqih adil) is established upon this basis; they are the vicegerents of the absent Imam, whose divine leadership is established by explicit designation, and who implicitly entrusted them with the guardianship of his followers. All of this authority, of course, is bestowed by Almighty God who has absolute authority and guardianship over all of creation.

In rejecting the explicit appointment of a successor to the Prophet, Sunni Jurists maintain that there are several means by which a caliph may be elected, which means there is no unique way to legitimize political power. Instead, they accept the appointment of the first four caliphs following the Prophet's death as a religious source to sanction political authority. Consequently, according to Sunni interpretations, a caliph may be elected either by a few of the elites (e.g. some outstanding companions of the Prophet), by the explicit designation of his predecessor, or by an appointed council (shura).

The fact that many of the contemporary political positions of that time had been secured by coercion and military power, created a serious obstacle for the theory of caliphate and many Sunni scholars attempted to find a means to justify these authorities. For example, Al-Mawardi attempted to legitimize the authority of de facto rulers by designating them as government ministers (wazir) and commanders (amir), whom the caliph had to recognize.[14]

Finally, the third distinction arises, which is concerned with the qualities that a leader must possess. According to the doctrine of Shi'ism, an Imam is not merely a political leader; rather he is also a religious leader who undertakes the exposition of divine sciences. Like the Prophet, he must embody the highest moral and intellectual qualities, such as immunity from sin and infallible knowledge. However, there is a wide-ranging disagreement amongst Sunni scholars regarding the characteristics of a caliph. Commonly, they do not believe that a candidate must be sinless, or enjoy infallible knowledge. In some cases, justice and fairness are not considered necessary, and obedience is required of even an unjust or oppressive tyrant. Al-Ghazzali says:

> *An evil doing and barbarous Sultan, so long as he is supported by military force (shawka) so that he can only be deposed with difficulty, and that the attempt to*

---

[14] Antony Black, *The History of Islamic Political Thought*, p.88.

> *depose him would create unendurable civil strife,*
> *must necessarily be left in possession, and obedience*
> *must be rendered to him.*[15]

A general and significant feature of Sunni political thinking is that there is no procedure for the people to depose an unjust ruler. Rather, the grounds on which he may be removed are considerably reduced. For instance, Al-Baghdadi (d. 1037) said that allegiance (bay'a) might only be revoked on grounds of heresy, incapacitation, imprisonment or serious injustice; although the latter is not accepted as a cause for disobedience by most Sunni scholars.[16]

Although Imami political theory does not require a wali al-faqih to be sinless or infallible, it does mention characteristics such as justice, fairness and expertise in jurisprudence as necessary qualities. This is because the jurists (fuqaha) are not only moral and legal experts they are also representatives of the hidden Imam.

The Meaning of Wilayat al-Faqih

The words "wali" and "wilayat" have the same root (w-l-y). From it's primary meaning of "to be near or close to someone or something", is derived the general meanings "to be in charge", "to govern" and "to exercise authority". In Islamic juristic (fiqh) terminology, the term "wilayat" has several usages. Some of these are as follow:

---

[15] *Ibid.*, p. 104.
[16] *Ibid.*, p. 85.

1. Wilayat al-Qaraba

is type of authority (*Wilayat*) is given to a father or
ernal grandfather over minors and those who are insane
en after the age of adolescence). This authority to act as a
rdian is based on relationship.

2. Wilayat al-Qada'

According to Imami Jurisprudence, the infallible Imam
originally possessed the sole authority to judge amongst the
people based upon God's law and revelation. At this time,
however, a just and capable faqih may undertake this
responsibility with the Imam's permission.

3. Wilayat al-Hakim

In this case, authority is given to a regular administrator of
justice (hakim), to supervise the interests of a person who is
unable to take care of his own affairs; such as a fool or an
insane person. Whoever does not have a guardian (wali),
jurists say: al-hakim is the guardian of those who have no
guardian.

4. Wilayat al-Mutlaqa (The Absolute Authority)

According to textual evidences, such as verse 6 of Chapter
33 of the Qur'an, Imami scholars believe that the Prophet
and Imams have divine authority over the people. The verse
states that the Prophet has more rights over the believers
than they have over themselves; thus his discretionary
authority is effective amongst the people. This same
authority, according to Shia beliefs, is also bestowed upon
the Imams.

5. Wilayat al-Usuba

According to Sunni jurists, this authority is connected to inheritance; it encompasses a class of inheritors. This category of wilayat is not accepted by Imami scholars.

According to Imami doctrine, absolute authority (wilayat al-Mutlaqa al-Elahiya) remains with the Absent Imam, even during his greater occultation. Therefore, in order to exercise authority, every just and capable faqih requires the sanction of the Imam, who is in turn designated by God as the possessor of absolute authority and guardianship.

Although all Imami scholars generally agree upon the doctrine of Vicegerency (Niyabat) that emphasizes the role of capable jurists as deputies of the Absent Imam, who are entrusted with a degree of his authority. However, the crucial issue is the scope and extent of this vicegerency and in which affairs the jurists have authority.

In order to clarify the dimensions of this discussion, it is necessary to examine the traditional roles and functions that qualified jurists undertake as deputies of the Imam.

i) Making a Decree (Al-Ifta)

With regards to guidance in rulings and religious duties, it is necessary for those who lack sufficient knowledge of Islamic law and the legal system (shari'a) to refer to the opinions of a jurist (faqih). The jurist who issues legal and juridical decrees is known as a "Marja'a taqleed", and the term meaning to follow or imitate their opinion is "taqleed".

There is no disagreement amongst scholars regarding the application of this function by a well-qualified jurist. After all when a person has questions on a particular topic, it is only natural for them to refer these to an expert in this field, not only in the sphere of religion, but in all aspects of life. For this reason, although the jurist must possess certain qualities to assume this role, there is no need for the express permission of an Imam. In other words this function should not be mentioned as an example of the Imam 's authority and a type of wilayat.

ii) To Judge (Al-Qada)

It is legally established that a just faqih is able to mediate disputes and judge in legal cases. Imamis believe that this function (wilayat al-qada or al-hukuma) is encompassed within the Imam's divine authority. Hence, only those who have his permission may assume this role. Imam as-Sadiq (pbuh) referred to the administration of justice (hukuma) as a constitutional right and duty of the Imam:

> *Beware of the Hukuma (administration of justice). Indeed, al-Hukuma belongs to the Imam who is knowledgeable in matters of judicial decisions (qada) and who is the just one (al-adil) among the Muslims, like the Prophet or his legatee.*[17]

Imami jurists commonly agree that this responsibility (wilayat al-qada) is entrusted to the just faqih as a deputy of the Imam.

---

[17] Abdulaziz Sachedina, *The Just Ruler*, Oxford University Press, 1988, p. 129.

Hisbiya Affairs (Al-Umur al-Hisbiya)

The Prophet (pbuh) said:

> *The sultan is the wali of the one who does not have a wali.*[18]

According to this hadith, the sultan is the guardian (wali) of those who need a guardian to for a particular reason. For example, when the father of a minor or an insane person dies. Imami jurists extend this role to a set of affairs that require an authorized guardian to oversee them; these are known as al-umur al-hisbiya, and include religious endowments, inheritance and funerals (as well as those mentioned above). Although all Imami jurists accept the legality and necessity of this role, they disagree as to whether or not he is appointed by the shari'a or because he is naturally the best suited for the role. Some maintain that there is no expressed permission stemming from Islamic traditions to justify the authority of a jurist in such cases (hisbah). However, though the shari'a is silent, this does not mean that issues of hisbah do not need to be attended to. And a faqih who has knowledge of the shari'a and is just and pious, logically has priority over all others in these cases.

These three functions only form a fraction of the Imam's authority; in the history of Imami Shi'ism, marja'aiyya (authorative reference) has largely been restricted to these central roles (especially the first). However, the religious authority and duties of an Imam as a guardian (wali) extend far beyond the three functions mentioned above. Those who

---

[18] Muhammad Baqer Majlesi, *Behar al-Anwar* (110 volumes), Tehran, 1985, Kitab al-Elm, Chapter 1, Hadith 29.

believe in universal vicegerency (wilayat al-amma) maintain that the role of the faqih is not restricted to merely a few religious duties, but rather he has the same authority as the Imam. He has the right and duty to lead the Shia community and undertake the full function and responsibilities of an infallible Imam.

In addition to the administration of justice (wilayat al-qada) and 'hisbah', the Imam also has the right to exercise governmental, juridical and economic duties. The political nature of these duties consequently implies that the Imam is the leader and ruler of Muslim society (wilayat al-siyasiyya). Those who advocate wilayat al-amma extend the scope of the faqih's authority to the following duties:

1 - Political- Devotional (Ibady) Orders and Prayers

Imami fuqaha emphasize that performing certain religious ceremonies, such as leading the prayers of Eid al-Adha and Eid al-Fitr, in addition to the prayer of Jum'ah (Friday), can only be lead by an Imam or one who has been designated by Him. This view presupposes that leading the prayers is a political-religious position and a function of the true Imam. For instance, Shaykh al-Mufid[19] says:

It is well established that every imperfect being needs someone who can discipline him so that he will refrain from evil acts...He should also be the one who

---

[19] Muhammad ibn Muhammad ibn al-Nu'man, known as Mufid is one of the greatest Imami faqih and theologian. He was born in Dujal, some sixty miles from Baghdad, in the year 949 or 950AD. His basic and elementary training and studies was under his father. He went to Baghdad at the age of twelve. Among his books in fiqh is al-Muqni'a, on which Tusi wrote a commentary-Tahdhib al-Ahkam (one of the four major books of Imami Shi'ism).

> *will protect Islamic territory and will assemble the*
> *people in order to convene the Jum'ah and the Eid*
> *prayers.* [20]

In addition, the formal affirmation of the new moon for religiously important occasions (e.g. Shawal for Eid al-Fitr), requires the endorsement of a just and capable Imam (Imam adil).

2 - Legal Punishment (Hudud)

It is established in Islamic traditions that the application of legal punishment (hudud) requires the sanction of an Imam. Considering that some categories of legal punishment involve pain, injury or death, whoever is entrusted with this duty, must have the legitimate authority to deal with these issues. The administration of justice and application of legal punishment obviously require political authority, otherwise they are impossible to enforce both legitimately and consistently. Functions that involve the administration of justice, such as determining compensation (diyat), dividing inheritance and affairs such as retaliation (qisas), also belong to the Imam.

3 - Islamic Taxes

The collection and distribution of taxes is one of the most important functions of any government, therefore those who have the right to fulfill this duty also have political authority (wilayat al-siyasiyya). Sunni jurists generally maintain that a sultan (deputy), who has political power, can receive taxes such as zakat. Imami fuqaha, on the other hand, believe that

---

[20] Shaykh Al-Mufid, *Al-Ershad*, Tehran, 1972, p. 674.

the Imam has the sole entitlement to receive Islamic taxes (zakat, sadaqa, kharaj) and decide how they should be spent.

4 - Jihad (Holy War) and Defense

Unlike a number of Sunni jurists, who consider fighting unbelievers for the expansion of the Islamic state as a form of "Jihad". The scope of Jihad is not so broad amongst Imami jurists who, in order to prevent the abuse of this concept by corrupt political authorities, insist that the permission of the Imam is a necessary condition for Jihad. Shaykh Tusi says:

> It is imperative that the Imam should be the one to commence Jihad against unbelievers (kuffar).[21]

Sachedina explains why there is no justification for Jihad without permission of the Imam in the Imami point of view:

> The original purpose of Jihad, then according to the Imami, was not preserved under the Caliphate. What had caused the Jihad to drift away from the Qur'anic purpose was the coming to power of unjust and unrighteous authority claiming to undertake Jihad in the name of God. Of the two main purposes of Jihad, namely to call upon the people to respond to God's guidance, and to protect the basic welfare of the community, the first purpose, according to all the Imami Jurists, required the presence of the just Imam or the person deputized by such an authority. This

---

[21] Muhammad ibn Hassan Tusi, *Al-Mabsut fi Fiqh al-Imamiya*, Tehran, 1958, Volume 2, p. 9.

*was to guarantee that Jihad against unbelievers was
undertaken strictly for the cause of God.*[22]

These four categories of authority and function introduce an
essential issue in determining the scope of a vicegerent 's
authority. If an Imam has delegated his authority and duties
entirely to a just and capable jurist (faqih) as his deputy
during the period of greater occultation, the guardianship
(wilayat) of fuqaha would be universal (amma). Universal
guardianship implies that the Islamic society is in need of a
wali to lead and organize it's affairs, regardless of whether
an infallible Imam is present or not.

Wilayat al-faqih can be defined as an authority entrusted to
learned fuqaha so that they may direct and advise the
Muslim ummah in the absence of an infallible Imam. This
authority is derived from the Imam, who is al-Hujjah (the
proof of God), therefore it is incumbent to obey their
commands as the only legitimate authority. However, there
remains some ambiguity surrounding the scope of the
authority (wilayat) that has been delegated to the fuqaha.

The concept of wilayat encompasses many degrees of
authority. The highest form of authority (wilayat) bestowed
upon the faqih is the universal type (wilayat al-amma),
whereas the most basic form is embodied in the authority to
undertake 'hisbah' and 'qada' (the administration of justice).
Some people make the mistake of assuming that wilayat al-
faqih refers only to the universal authority, when in fact it
refers to the total scope of the scholar's vicegerency in the
absence of an infallible Imam.

---

[22] Abdulaziz Sachedina, *The Just Ruler*, p. 110.

Some Misconceptions

At this point, it is necessary to address two common misconceptions surrounding wilayat al-faqih. Many people erroneously assume that it is something new and in essence distinguishable from the traditional status of marja'aiyya. This misunderstanding is caused by a lack of attention to the definitions of and the relationship between 'wilayat' and 'marja'aiyya' and the distinction between 'fatwa' and 'hukm' (the commands of faqih as wali)

The role of a marja'a taqleed is widely considered to be solely a juridical authority to whom the Muslim community may refer to in the case of religious questions and commandments concerning the practical side of Islam (fiqhi questions). However, this definition is not comprehensive; it concentrates exclusively on one of the legitimized functions of a jurist, while overlooking the others. As we mentioned previously, the faqih has at least three significant functions; as an expert in Islamic law and jurisprudence, he is entitled to undertake 'ifta'. However, as an appointed deputy of the Imam, he has the authority (wilayat) to exercise 'hisbah' and 'qada'. Accordingly, every faqih is entitled to issue a decree (fatwa) and, at the same time, to be appointed as 'wali' to undertake specific functions. When the jurist administers justice or acts as a legal guardian to a 'mawla alayh' (someone who is without a legal guardian) he is known as a 'wali' or 'hakim al-shar' and when he is referred to in religious (fiqh) issues, he is usually called 'marja'a taqleed'. A necessary distinction must be made between a 'fatwa' (decree) issued by a faqih in his capacity as a religious authority (marja'a) and a 'hukm' (order) issued by him as a wali and 'hakim' (guardian or ruler).

A 'fatwa' is classified as a decree issued by the jurist based on his deductions from Islamic sources. He attempts to determine the position of the shari'a and divine commandments with regards to a specific issue, in which his opinion will be adopted by those who submit to his religious authority (muqalid). On the other hand, a 'hukm' is an order issued by a wali regarding a particular set of circumstances, the Islamic legal system and interests of the Muslims. Therefore, it is not merely due to his deduction from a religious source, though he must respect the shari'a when issuing a hukm. The hukm is intended to effectively organize and resolve difficulties within Muslim society.

Another key issue concerns the relationship between the first function of the faqih, which is ifta, and the other duties that are subject to his wilayat (guardianship). Theoretically, these two elements seem independent and entirely separable from one another, but can they really be disassociated?

Suppose that there were one hundred just and capable scholars, who fulfilled the qualities required to assume the role of wali and marja'a. It is not obligatory upon all of them as an 'individual duty' (wajib al-ainy) to assume responsibility for all three functions of a faqih? The answer is negative. Performing these functions is a 'sufficient necessary' (wajib al-kefai), which means that if a number of them were to undertake these three duties, then the others would no longer be obliged to issue a 'fatwa', to judge or to act as a guardian (if the others are meeting the requirements of the community). In conclusion, although ever faqih potentially could become marja'a and wali, only a few of them will effectively assume these functions.

At its highest degree, the universal vicegerency of the jurist (wilayat al-amma) also encompasses political authority (wilayat al-siyasiyya). Some adversaries of the doctrine maintain that the meaning of 'wilayat' (guardianship) in Imami jurisprudence is essentially incompatible with political authority. They argue that, according to the Islamic legal system, 'guardianship' requires the existence of a 'mawla alayh' (one who is need of a guardian), which in definition refers to those who are impotent in their affairs, whereas political authority cannot presuppose that the subjects of a government fall into this category. Therefore the guardianship of a faqih is limited in scope and has no connection to political authority.[23]

The term 'wilayat' is used in two cases in the Qur'an and Islamic traditions; firstly there are circumstances when a 'mawla alayh' is unable to discharge his or her own affairs (in cases of insanity, incapacity or immaturity) – this is umur al-hisbah. The second involves the authority of the Imam to administer justice (wilayat al-qada) and collect taxes. However this case does not presume any disability on behalf of the 'mawla alayh'. Although people are generally able to manage their own private affairs, there remain matters in every society that require the existence of a reliable, credible and just authority to undertake and supervise them. The Qur'an introduces Allah, the Prophet and (according to the Shia perspective) the Imams as guardians (wali) over the believers. Clearly these verses consider the believers (mawla alayh) in need of divine guidance and leadership, and not as impotents who need supervision in all of their personal affairs.

---

[23] Mehdi Haery Yazdi, *Hekmat wa Hokumat*, p. 177.

The authority and guardianship of the faqih is a social duty, which is delegated to them. Consequently it neither gives them an increased status in humanity, nor decreases the status of people who admit the guardianship of a just and capable faqih. Imam Khomeini says:

> *By authority we mean governance, the administration of the country and the implementation of the sacred laws of the shari'a. This constitutes a serious and difficult duty but does not earn anyone an extraordinary status or raise him above the level of common humanity. In other words, authority here has the meaning of a government, administration and execution of law, contrary to what many people believe, it is not a privilege but a grave responsibility.*[24]

The Historical Background

Universal guardianship (wilayat al-amma) is undoubtedly the most fundamental element of Imami political doctrine in the era of occultation (ghaibat). Therefore, it is essential to understand what position the most learned Imami jurists have historically adopted regarding this concept. Moreover, it is often speciously conceived that wilayat al-amma is a new development in Islamic thought, which has no origins amongst the early Imami jurists. However, a brief survey of its historical background in Imami jurisprudence reveals not only the weakness of this supposition, but it also illustrates that wilayat al-amma is a concept widely endorsed by many outstanding jurists.

---

[24] *Islam and Revolution*, pp. 62-63.

When examining a historical account of scientific studies, it is easy to overlook two important points. Firstly, we often assume that our predecessors approached a problem from the same perspective and with the same clarity as we do. However, this expectation is rarely validated with regards to debates on subjects such as politics, which encompass various dimensions that each constitutes an area of specialized research (such as philosophy and ideology). Therefore it is hardly correct to suppose that political thinkers in the past necessarily followed the same problem or methodology as contemporary intellectuals. Secondly, although scholars today are freely able to write and express their own ideas, this often leads us to mistakenly expect that the social and political climate was the same for previous scholars, who in fact lived under illegitimate and often oppressive governments. They were thus often forced to practice precautionary dissimulation (taqiyyah) and were unable to explicitly state their opinions.

There are two strands of thought amongst the supporters of wilayat al-amma. There are those who explicitly and directly insist that the vicegerency of a faqih is universal. While on the other hand, some scholars maintain that a learned jurist may be entrusted to undertake a number of duties in addition to the primary three of ifta, qada and hisbah.

The latter of these two opinions usually occurs in the early period of Shia jurisprudence. Until the emergence of the Safawid dynasty in Iran, the Shia community existed as a minority, without political power. Hence, the universal authority of a faqih, ruling and political jurisprudence had very little bearing on the circumstances of the Shia, which is why the fuqaha devoted less attention to discussing matters of political theory and the duties of a ruler.

When taking into account the opinions of these learned scholars, it is important to recognize that they not only state their personal opinion (ijtihad) concerning the scope a jurist's guardianship, but also maintain that this opinion is in accordance with the general consensus (ijmaa) of the Imami fuqaha. This reinforces the assumption that jurists who were historically silent regarding political issues, such as governance and universal authority, remained so due to the social and political circumstances of the time (taqiyyah).

Regarding the first school of thought regarding wilayat al-amma, one of the most important Imami jurists, al-Muhaqqiq al-Karaki[25] says:

> *Imami fuqaha have consensus on the point that the fully qualified faqih, known as a mujtahid, is the deputy (nayib) of the infallible ones (peace be upon them) in all the affairs attendant upon the deputyship. Hence, it is obligatory to refer to him in litigation and accept his verdict. If necessary, he can sell the*

---

[25] Ali ibn Abd al-A'l who is better known as Muhaqqiq al-Karaki or even the second Muhaqqiq-researcher- (after Helli who is famous as the first Muhaqqiq in fiqh) died in 937/1530. He was originally from Jabal Amel, south Lebanon. He like the first and the second shahid (martyr) completed his studies in Sham and Iraq and different centers of Sunni learning before coming to Iran during the reign of the Safavid denasty (Shah Tahmasb). In this period of Iran's history the authority of Imami scholars had been increased and Karaki had a great status in administration of justice. He established a great seminary (Hawza) in Qazvin and Isfahan consequently Iran once again became center of Imami jurisprudence. One of his famous books in fiqh is 'Jame ul-Maqasid' which is a commentary on the book of Allama al Helli-Qawaid.

property of the party who refuses to pay what he is due...rather, if it were not for the wilayat al-amma many of the Shia community's affairs and needs would remain undone.[26]

Shaykh Muhammad Hassan[27], The author of an encyclopedic work in Imami fiqh, 'Jawahir al-Kalam' writes:

...carrying out Islamic sentences and implementing religious injunctions is obligatory at the era of occultation. Being the deputy of the Imam (Pbuh) in many cases rests with the fuqaha. The faqih's social status is the same as the Imam. There is no difference between him and the Imam (Pbuh) in this respect. [The verdict of] Our fuqaha on this issue [is] unanimous; in their works they frequently underscore the idea of referring to a guardian/governor (hukm) who is the agent and representative of the Absent Imam. If the fuqaha are not to have the general vicegerency, all the affairs of the Shia will remain unattended. Those who surprisingly raise objections about the wilayat al-amma of the faqih, then seem to be ignorant of jurisprudence and the words of the infallible ones; they have not pondered these words and their meanings[28].

---

[26] The articles (al-Rasayel) of Mhaqqiq al-Karaki, edited by Muhammad al-Hassun, the first collection (Al-Ressala fi al-Salat ul-Jom'a), Qom, 1409AH, pp, 142, 143

[27] He was of Arab descent and died in 1849. Shaikh Muhammad spent thirty years to complete his great work (al-Jawahir) which the last print of the book in Iran includes forty three volumes. It is a commentary on the book of Muhaqqiq al-Helli (al-Sharay').

[28] Muhammad Hassan, *Jawahir al-Kalam*, Tehran: Dar al-Kotob al-Islamiya, 1398AH, Volume 21, pp. 396-397.

Hajj Aqa Reza Hamedani[29] also maintains that wilayat al-amma is a unanimous concept amongst Shia jurists:

> *In any case, there is no doubt that the fuqaha of integrity (Jame al-Sharayeti), who have all the perfect, necessary qualities to undertake the vicegerency are the deputy of the Imam of the time in such matters. Our fuqaha have testified to this in their works. Their statements indicate that they regard the vicegerency of faqih in all matters as indisputable so much so that some of them have taken consensus (Ijmaa) to be the pivotal proof of the faqih's general guardianship (neyabat al-amma).[30]*

As we discussed earlier, many jurists attribute duties to the faqih that require him to be entrusted with universal authority. The evidences regarding the appointment of a faqih as a deputy of them Imam cover many chapters of fiqh, the explanation of which would require many pages. However, in the interests of our discussion, we will examine only a few of them here. Shaykh al-Mufid (334-413 A.H) asserts that the application of legal punishment (hudud) is one of the key functions of a faqih:

> *It is the duty of the ruler of Islam (Sultan al-Islam) who is appointed by Almighty God to implement hudud. Sultan al-Islam is the infallible Imams from Muhammad's (Pbuh) family or the rulers and governors (Hukm) who are designated by them. They*

---

[29] Died in 1904 the author of some significant books in Imami jurisprudence such as 'Mesbah al-faqih'.
[30] Hajj Aqa Reza Hamedani, *Mesbah al-Faqih*, The Chapter of Khums, Volume 14, p. 291.

have entrusted this duty to the fuqaha where possible.[31]

Early Imami jurists applied titles such as 'sultan al-Islam', 'hukm' and 'wali' to the Imams. Many of these, such as sultan al-Islam, originally belong to the infallibles (Prophet and Imams) and so seldom apply to others. However, the majority of them also refer to those who are the appointed deputies of the Imam as well. For instance, Fakhr al-Muhaqqiqeen[32] says:

The meaning of 'hakim' here is the just ruler (al-Sultan al-adil) or his deputy. When there is no access to the Sultan or his particular deputy, it is the role of a well-qualified faqih...so when the author (Allamah Hilli) says "when there is no hakim" he means by 'hakim' all these three [above].[33]

Muhaqqiq al-Karaki also endorses the above interpretations of 'hakim'. He writes:

Al-hakim refers to an infallible Imam or his particular deputy. In the era of occultation, the Imam's general deputy (al-nayb al-amm) is the well qualified jurist...It should be noted that when the fuqaha use the term (hakim) unconditionally, it exclusively refers to a well qualified faqih.[34]

---

[31] Muhammad ibn Nu'man (al-Mofid), *Al-Moqni'a*, p. 810.

[32] He is Muhammad the son of Allama Helli. His famous book on fiqh is 'Eidhah al-Fawaid' which is a commentary of his father 's book (al-Qawaid). He died in 771AH.

[33] Fakhr al-Muhaqqiqeen, *Eidhah al-Fawaid*, Volume 2, p.624.

[34] *Al-Jami ul-Maqasid*, Volume 11, Kitab ul-wasaya, pp. 266-267.

It is important to remember that 'judge' is not synonymous with 'hakim'. This is because the application and enforcement of legal punishments, in the view of Imami scholars, is delegated to the governor (hakim) and not the judge (qada). Hafs ibn Qiyas asked Imam as-Sadiq (pbuh): "Who is in charge of punishment, the ruler or a judge?" To which the Imam replied: "The application of hudud is due to he whom has hukm (who governs)".[35]

This distinction clearly indicates that the application of legal punishments (hudud) requires full political authority; which in turn necessitates universal guardianship (wilayat al-amma). A view that is supported by many Imami jurists, such as al-Karaki:

> *The reliable well qualified Jurist who can issue legal decisions is designated by the Imam. Accordingly his rulings are effective and it is obligatory to assist him in the administration of al-Hudud and al-qada, among the people. It is not proper to say that the Jurist is designated for administration of Justice and for giving legal decisions only, and that the Jum'ah prayer is a matter outside the scope of these two responsibilities. Such an opinion is extremely weak because the jurist has been appointed as al-hakim, by the Imams, which is well documented in the traditions.[36]*

As we discussed, the Jum'ah prayer is a political function, which, in the view of the Imami jurists, belongs to the Imam. Therefore, every Imami jurist who believes that the fuqaha

---

[35] Shaikh Hur al-A'meli, Muhammad ibn Hassan, *Wasael al-Shi'a*, Qom: Ahl ul-Bait Institution, 1412 AH, Volume18, p. 220.
[36] *The Just Ruler*, p. 196.

are able to fulfill this function during the period of occultation (ghaibat), would also have admit to the validity of wilayat al-amma.

Moreover, if the authority of the faqih is not confined to the role of legal arbitration and guardianship, then the Imami mujtahid may say that the fuqaha have the authority to collect Islamic taxes, which is an obvious indication of universal authority. The first shaheed (martyr)[37] says:

> It is said that it is obligatory to give 'zakat' to the jurist during the occultation if he asks for it himself or through his agents because he is the deputy of the Imam, just as the collector of the taxes is. Rather, however, it is more appropriate to state that his vicegerency on behalf of the Imam is applicable in all those matters in which the Imam himself has authority; whereas the collector is the agent of the Imam only in a particular function.[38]

The second shaheed[39] also believes that the Islamic taxes (zakat) should be delivered to the Imam, or to the trusted

---

[37] He is Muhammad ibn Makki who was born in south Lebanon-Jabal Amil- in 734AH. Fakhr ul-Mohaqqeqin was one of his teachers. He was martyred as a result of a fatwa issued by a Maliki jurist, supported by Shafei, in the year 786.He has written some significant books in fiqh such as 'Luma'h', 'Durrus', 'Dhikra' and 'Bayan'.

[38] Translated in 'The Just Ruler' from *Jawaher al- Kalam*, Volume 15, p. 422.

[39] Shaikh Zain ul-Din is one of greatest Shi'a jurists. He was born in 911 AH and was expert in Sunni jurisprudence as well. One of his important works is a commentary on the first Shaheed's work (Luma'h) and it is a strange coincidence that the author and the commentator both were executed and martyred.

Jurist during occultation. He later explains why the zakat should be given to the faqih:

> *One must bear in mind that he (the faqih) is appointed in the interest of the public, and if he were to be dishonest there would occur harm to those who were entitled to receive the zakat.* [40]

In concluding the historical background of wilayat al-amma, it is necessary to re-emphasize that this doctrine is widely supported by later Imami jurists. Who, explicitly and more clearly than their predecessors, support the universal authority of a faqih. A number of these jurists, and their works, are as follows:

- Mullah Ahmad al-Naraqi, in his work Awaid al-Ayyam, chapter 'Wilayat al-fuqaha', Page 529.
- Sayyid Mirfattah al-Maraqi in al-Anavin Page.355. Al-Bahr al-Ulum in Bolqatol al-faqih, Volume 3, Page.231.
- Shaykh Abd al-Allah Mamaqani in Risala al-Anam fi hukm e-amwal al-Imam, Page 14.
- Mirza al-Nayyini in 'Al-Makaseb wa al-Bai', edited by Shaykh Muhammad Amali, Volume 1, Page 336.
- Sayyid Muhammad Hussain Borujerdi in al-Badr al-Zahir fi salat al-Jum'a, Page 71.
- Sayyid Muhammad Reza Gulpaayigani in 'al-Hedaya ela man Lahu al-Wilayat, Page 46.

---

[40] *Ibid.*

Multiplicity in Wilayat

Although according to Imami political doctrine, authority (wilayat) is bestowed upon a deputy (wali) by the infallible Imam, there is an important distinction between the specific designation of a deputy and the 'general' designation of a number of deputies. While there was an explicit nomination for each of the Imams to undertake leadership, and for the vicegerency of the four deputies during the minor absence, the guardianship of the jurists during the greater absence is a 'general' designation. This means that no faqih is exclusively appointed as 'wali' and deputy; all Imami jurists who are just and qualified in fiqh (ijtihad) have the right to exercise the Imam's authority as his deputies. Accordingly, universal authority has been entrusted to many jurists in every age and generation. Inevitably, this multiplicity means that the Imami theory of leadership could be confronted by the problem of disturbances and conflict, as polarization between various sources of decision-making naturally results in differences and chaos. In the context of the present discussion, it is important to assess how the universal theory of guardianship might address such issues.

In most cases, multiplicity does not present any serious problem regarding the functions of the fuqaha. It is unrealistic to insist that all cases of 'hisbah' need to be undertaken by a single jurist. Likewise, there is no reason to expect uniformity in 'Marja'aiyya' and the administration of justice. The fundamental difficulty arising from multiplicity, however, is that of political authority and leadership (wilayat al-siyasiyya).

The best way to approach this concern is to consider the status of the fuqaha who are entitled to political authority.

Wilayat al-faqih defines the criteria required of a ruler, and maintains that anyone who fulfils these qualities has the right to govern. In principal, authority (wilayat) does not demand any extra conditions. However, to be practically applied such authority requires suitable political circumstances and the recognition of the people. According to Imami doctrine, if Muslims appoint a just and capable jurist as their leader, then other fuqaha are obliged to support him and obey his orders, so long as he fulfils the qualities of wilayat. This situation is comparable to the relationship between judges; when one is responsible for a specific case, though other judges are entitled in principal to perform the same role, they have no right to interfere in his judgment. Shia traditions discuss the appointment of the fuqaha as deputies of the Imam, but they do not endorse or design a particular method to acknowledge or elect one or more jurists who possess the wilayat. Article 107 of the constitution of the Islamic Republic of Iran, suggests the following process:

> *The task of appointing the leader shall be vested with the experts elected by the people. The experts will review and consult among themselves concerning all the religious men possessing the qualifications specified in Article 5 and 109. In the event they find one of them better versed in Islamic regulations or in political and social issues or possessing general popularity...they shall elect him as the leader.*

The Dominion of the Wali al-Faqih

When considering that wilayat al-faqih represents the keystone of Imami political doctrine in the Era of Greater Occultation, it is essential that we assess the scope and domain of its authority. For our present subject, we must take into account the power of other religious authorities amongst the Imamis; the marja'ai. Does the wali al-faqih have authority (wilayat) only over those who accept him as their marja'a, or those who imitate marja'ai that support the idea of wilayat al-amma?

Aside from the relationship between the wali al-faqih as a political leader and other fuqaha as marja'ai, it is also important to gauge the authority of the wali al-faqih regarding the shari'a. Is he only able to issue orders within the framework of the Islamic legal system, or is he fully authorized to make decisions even if they contradict the shari'a? In other words, is his license as a ruler defined by the shari'a, or is his authority above the shari'a and therefore absolute?

We can structure our analysis around two significant aspects; the people's respect for his orders, and his respect for the Islamic legal system (shari'a). However, before proceeding with this discussion, we should review two important points.

Firstly, unlike Imamate, which is considered as a fundamental aspect of belief (aqueeda) in Shi'ism, wilayat al-faqih is a juridical (fiqh) subject matter. What distinguishes a fiqhi discussion from a theological (kalam) one, is that while the latter concerns issues of belief (disagreement upon which would render an individuals belief imperfect), the former is legal and thus subject to divergence of opinion even amongst the scholars of a particular Islamic sect (as disagreement in these issues does not invalidate belief). Hence, there can be disagreement on the universal authority of the jurist, as a juridical (fiqh) discussion and such disputes are not concerned with faith (iman).

Secondly, a necessary distinction must be made between a fatwa (religious decree) and hukm (order). As previously stated, a decree, deduced from Islamic sources and issued by a qualified faqih – fatwa – is valid and reliable for those who refer to him as their marja'a taqleed (religious authority), thus it is binding upon them to obey his fatwa. However, those who refer to other scholars as religious authorities are not obliged to observe this ruling. But an order (hukm) issued by the wali al-faqih is binding upon all Muslims, not merely his followers, regardless of how far his political authority might reach. Therefore, a command issued by a jurist as wali al-qada in the administration of justice is obligatory for everyone, even other fuqaha, because the just and capable jurist is appointed as hakim (wali). This opinion is supported by a tradition from Imam as-Sadiq (pbuh), in which Umar ibn Hanzala transmits that the Imam prohibited his followers (Shia) to recourse to a tyrannical or illegitimate authority (taghut) to resolve their affairs. Instead they are obliged to refer to one who relates the traditions of the Ahlul-Bayt and knows what is lawful and prohibited (i.e. a faqih). Imam as-Sadiq (pbuh) said:

I have appointed him a hakim over you. If such a person orders (judges) according to our ruling and the person concerned does not accept it, then he has shown contempt for the ruling of God and rejects us;

*and he who rejects us, actually rejects Allah and such
a person is close to association [Shirk] with Allah.[41]*

In this tradition, Imam as-Sadiq (pbuh) addresses the role of
a just faqih (hakim) who has been entrusted with authority
by the infallible Imam. According to this hadith, the people
are not allowed to recourse to an illegitimate or oppressive
authority for the resolution of their problems. Instead they
are required to refer to the wali (hakim) and obey his
decisions, regardless of whether or not he is their marja'a
taqleed.

Such as solution, however, hardly seems convincing for
those who do not accept wilayat al-amma. One might argue
that the wali al-faqih issues commands (hukm) based upon
his own opinion (fatwa) that the authority of the jurist is
universal (wilayat al-amma), while according to the view of
another marja'a the scope of a jurists authority is limited and
he is not designated to undertake political affairs. According
to this view, the tradition of Umar ibn Hanzala and others do
not include these kinds of orders.

However, this reasoning presents obvious problems that
extend far beyond the governmental orders (hukm) of a
jurist. For instance, when administering justice (wilayat al-
qada) a faqih issues an order according to his own religious
decree (fatwa), however there is no excuse for people to
disregard or disobey his command on the grounds that he is
not their marja'a. This is because the authority to judge (al-
qada) and the authority to issue decrees (al-ifta) are
independent of one another, thus the role of the judge cannot

---

[41] Muhammad ibn Hassan al-Tusi, *Tahzib al-Ahkam*, Kitab ul-Qad'a,
Volume 6, p. 218, Hadith 514.

be infringed by the edict of a marja'a (as the marja'a is not the judge of that legal case). Furthermore, although the opponents of wilayat al-amma maintain that the designation of the faqih as the Imam's deputy does not extend to political authority (wilayat al-siyasiyya), this surely cannot imply that if the people elect a just and capable faqih as their leader, instead of an unjust person, that his leadership is some how illegitimate and people are free to disobey. We will return to this point in the next chapter when examining the authority of a faqih endorsed by 'hisbah'.

We noted earlier that the debate surrounding the authority of the wali al-faqih has two significant aspects. The second of these – the relationship between the faqih's commands and shari'a – is a very new discussion in Imami political jurisprudence, whereas the first aspect has been discussed by many fuqaha. Imam Khomeini was perhaps the first Imami faqih who explicitly and publicly discussed the connection between governmental orders (ahkam al-hukmati) and Islamic laws (ahkam al-shari'). He firmly advocated the absolute authority of the faqih (wilayat al-mutlaqa) and it is essential that we briefly clarify the definition of this term to avoid any misconceptions.

Al-Wilayat al-Mutlaqa

When one first encounters the idea that a jurist has an unlimited and absolute scope of authority (wilayat al-mutlaqa) in issuing governmental orders, it is easy to dismiss the model of political regime as "absolutism", which is defined in the Oxford political dictionary as follows:

Originally (1733) a theological concept referring to God's total power to decide about salvation. Extended

to politics indicating a regime in which the ruler
might legitimately decide anything. Usually applied to
monarchical regimes of the early modern period.[42]

This misinterpretation often leads to the false assumption
that there are no controls, restrictions or limitations upon the
powers of the faqih; his authority is unquestionable and he
can exert himself without regard to the demands of the
shari'a or the interests of his people. He has no duty to
respect the various kinds criteria and standards for his
governance. This is similar to a dictatorial model of
government, which is an absolute rule unrestricted by law,
constitution or other political, religious or moral factors
within the society and state. Clearly this interpretation of
absolute authority is not correct even when considering the
Prophet (pbuh) and the Infallible Imams. A faqih as wali
must meet certain criteria, one of which is justice. The above
conception of wilayat al-mutlaqa obviously contradicts the
idea of justice and such a person has no legitimate authority
(wilayat) over believers. The precise and correct
understanding of 'wilayat al-mutlaqa' has a close
relationship to discussion about the nature and various kinds
of 'command' (hukm) in Imami Jurisprudence, especially
the faqih's injunction as wali (al-hukm al-hukmati) and its
position among commands of shari'a.

i) Divine Laws (Al-Hukm as-Shari')

This refers to a set of rules and commands legislated by God
and expressed to people through the Prophet Muhammad
and his successors. Hukm al-Shari' is usually divided by

---

[42] Iain McLean, *The Concise Oxford Dictionary of Politics*, Oxford
University Press, 1996, p. 1.

Muslim Jurists into two divisions. The first part is called 'al-ahkam al-taklifi' which is the laws of duty and in turn divides into five divisions (obligation, prohibition, desirability, undesirability and permissibility or 'mubah'). The second part is called 'al-ahkam al-waz'i' which establishes specific relationships and situations (waz') that are subject to particular divine laws. For instance, marriage, ownership, purity and uncleanness are all situations that the Islamic legal system endorses and defines in particular matters and circumstances - usually al-hukm al-waz'i is subject to particular laws of duty. Divine laws also are called the first order laws (al-ahkam al-awaliya) because deeds and things by themselves - with no regard to temporal and unexpected accidents - are subjects to these laws and legislation of Islam.

ii) The Judge's Command (Al-Hukm al-Qadi)

Even though the legal decision of Judge (faqih) is issued with consideration of the shari'a and decrees of Islam, it is not a component of the shari'a. The judge's role is merely the execution (tanfidh) and application of Islamic law to juridical cases. In administration of justice, the faqih as Judge does not deduce Islamic laws rather he attempts to apply the most appropriate laws to the situation.

iii) Governmental Orders (Al-Hukm al-Wilai)

Supporters of universal authority (wilayat al-amma) do not restrict the orders (hukm) of the faqih to merely the administration of justice. As a hakim, the jurist may issue orders and it is incumbent upon all Muslims, even other fuqaha, to obey them. These include his edicts concerning the beginning of Ramadhan or the application of legal penalties (hudud). The best examples of orders that fall into this category are the governmental commands that the faqih may issue as the political leader of a society. The wali al-faqih may issue orders regarding situations that he recognizes as affecting the interests of Islam, Muslims and Islamic laws and values. A situation may arise in which the wali al-faqih can issue an order based on the interest (maslahat) of the people, even though in principal the action would not otherwise be compulsory in shari'a.

Two crucial questions arise regarding these orders. The first concerns the nature of the order; whether the governmental command is categorized as the 'first order' of the shari'a, or as the 'second order' (al-akham as-sanavy). The second question concerns the scope of such orders. A faqih may issue an obligatory or prohibitive order regarding matters that are considered permissible (mubah) and for which there is no prior obligation (for doing or not doing it) in Islamic law. However, a dispute arises about whether or not the faqih may issue orders that disregard the commands of the shari'a. Since the answer to the latter of these questions emerges from the former, it is necessary to explain what we mean by 'second order' commands (akham as-sanavy).

iv) Al-Hukm al-Awaly and al-Hukm al-Sanavy

The actions that we commit according to our free will are subject to one of the following categories in shari'a, namely obligation (wajib), prohibition (haraam), desirability (mustahab), undesirability (makruh) and simple permissibility (mubah). These 'first order' laws (al-ahkam al-awaly) are determined by the law giver (hakim) upon considering the essence and natural status of deeds and things. However, in exceptional situations and under circumstances in which people should not or cannot respect previous legislations, new rulings must be issued. These temporal laws are legislated according to the demands made by exceptional situations, and are called laws of 'the second order' (al-ahkam al-sanavy). They are secondary and temporal because people must revert to obeying the first order laws as soon as the exceptional circumstances return to normal. For instance, according to shari'a it is not permissible for Muslims to eat "carrion" (dead animals) or the meat of animals not ritually slaughtered. It is a first order command, but in a dire situation when a person has nothing to eat at all, God permits him or her to eat such meat, this permission is a second order law. The Qur'an says:

> He has only forbidden you what dies of itself, and blood, and flesh of swine, and that over which any other (name) other than (that of) Allah has been invoked, but whoever is driven to necessity, not desiring, nor exceeding the limit, no sin shall be upon him. [Chapter 2, Verse 173]

Fuqaha usually cite 'necessity' (ezterar), damage (zarar), distress and constriction (usr wa haraj), disorder of the Muslim's system (ekhtelal al-nidham) and compulsion (ekrah) as the major exceptional topics that demand and require second order laws, as reasons for reverting to laws of 'the second order'. The prevailing conception amongst Imami Jurists emphasizes that the governmental orders should be issued by the faqih only in one of the aforementioned exceptional situations because al-hukm al-hukmati is but a second order command.

When we consider this opinion, the answer to the second question – which is the relationship between governmental order and shari'a - is very clear. In a normal situation, the faqih has no right to issue orders in opposition to obligatory (either haraam or wajib) first order laws, even if the interest (maslahat) of the Muslims demands thus. In other words, interest as such cannot justify governmental orders when they are on the contrary with Islamic obligatory laws. However, situations in which the interest (maslahat) becomes so serious that ignorance of it could cause significant damage, distress and constriction or disorder, would allow the Wali al-faqih to issue these orders.

Ayatollah Khomeini, in a revolutionary view, stated that although the implementation of shari'a is very important, it is not the ultimate goal. Islamic laws (shari'a) serve as a means to achieve the primary aim embodied in the protection of Islam and the extension of Justice. For him the Islamic State is not merely one part of Islam amongst others, but it is Islam itself. Consequently the significance of Islamic laws is overshadowed by the significance of protecting the Islamic system and the interest (maslahat) of Islam. He expressed the view during his lectures in Iraq - the seminary of Najaf - years before the Islamic Revolution in Iran.

After the Islamic Revolution in Iran he explored this view more explicitly. In his famous letter to Ayatollah Khamenei (the current wali al-faqih), he insists that the authority of the Prophet and Imams to govern is not only a first order divine law but also it has priority over others such as praying, fasting, Hajj and so on. He writes:

> *The government or the absolute guardianship (al-wilayat al-mutlaqa) that is delegated to the noblest messenger of Allah is the most important divine laws and has priority over all other ordinances of the law. If the powers of the government restricted to the framework of ordinances of the law then the delegation of the authority to the Prophet would be a senseless phenomenon. I have to say that government is a branch of the Prophet's absolute Wilayat and one of the primary (first order) rules of Islam that has priority over all ordinances of the law even praying, fasting and Hajj...The Islamic State could prevent implementation of everything - devotional and non-devotional - that so long as it seems against Islam's interests.*[43]

Unlike conditional authority (wilayat al-muqayada) that restricts the right of the faqih for issuing governmental orders solely in permissibility cases (mubahat), wilayat al-mutlaqa, by definition, is a juridical view concerning the dominion of the just faqih to issue governmental orders even if it is in opposition with some obligatory Islamic laws.

As has become clear from the current discussion, the meaning of wilayat al-mutlaqa is totally different from 'absolutism' and the establishment of a totalitarian and dictatorial government. Some qualifications and conditions are essential for the wali al-faqih such as justice, piety and the necessary socio-political perspicacity. So, if he fails to meet one of them, he will be dismissed. In the constitution of Islamic Republic of Iran a group of experts elected by

---

[43] *Sahife' Noor* (letters and lectures of Ayatollah Khomeini), Volume 20, p. 170.

people supervise and control the leader. This constitution in article 111 says:

> *Whenever the leader becomes incapable of fulfilling his constitutional duties, or loses one of the qualifications mentioned in Article 5 and 109, or it becomes known that he did not possess some of the qualifications initially, he will be dismissed. The authority of determination in this matter with the experts specified in Article 108.*

As I indicated before, in Imami Political Jurisprudence 'wilayat al-mutlaqa' is a new term. Imami fuqaha usually use other terms such as 'wilayat al-amma' and 'neyabat al-Amma' to refer to the authority of faqih. Imam Khomeini applied the term publicly, then in 1990 it was enshrined in the constitution of Islamic Iran. Article 57 says:

> *The power of government in the Islamic Republic are vested in the legislature, the judiciary, and the executive powers, functioning under the supervision of the absolute religious leader and the leadership of the ummah.*

Wilayat al-Faqih and other Ideas of Guardianship

Perhaps Plato was the first political theorist who presented a comprehensive guardianship model of government. In the 'Republic', he states that political knowledge is a supreme art that aims to realize the good of the community. Attaining that knowledge requires serious training. Thus, men and women must be carefully selected and rigorously trained in order to achieve excellence in the art and science of politics. This serious training renders a few of them a class of 'true philosophers'[44], who deserve to rule the society. Therefore, the ideal Republic will come into existence if a class of guardians (Philosopher Kings) rules over it.

In the history of political thought, various interpretations of the guardianship model of the State have been suggested, Marxist-Leninism and all the political ideologies which believe in an organized group of revolutionaries, a vanguard, who possess the sufficient knowledge and commitment to overcome capitalism and to lead the working class to establish a socialist and non-class society are samples of the guardianship political theory.

Obviously, Shia political doctrine should be categorized as a guardianship model of government because it believes that only those who have specific qualifications (infallible ones or their deputies) have a right to govern the community. For Imamism the problem of leadership is not the question of people's elections. People have to accept and believe in divinely designated leadership just like the Prophecy in order for it to be practical. Since the fuqaha are generally designated as guardians, the role of the people within the period of occultation increases. They have a duty to acknowledge their governor among the fuqaha directly or through a selected group of fuqaha. Nevertheless, this participation of people does not render wilayat al-faqih a

---

[44] Grube maintains that Plato does not mean by 'philosopher king' the professional sense that at present the word 'philosopher' purport, he says: 'Plato does not mean that the world should be ruled by pale metaphysicians from the remoteness of their studies, he is maintaining that a statesman needs to be a thinker, a lover of truth, beauty and the Good, with a highly developed sense of values'.
Plato, *Plato's Republic*, G.M.A. Grube (tr), Indianapolis, 1974, n 13, p.133.

purely democratic and non-guardianship theory of State. Robert Dahl is quite right when he states that:

No single interpretation can do justice to the variations among the many different visions of guardianship.[45]

However, what he mentions at the beginning of his discussion could be recognized as the central point of the vision of guardianship:

The assumption by democrats that ordinary people are qualified, they, (advocates of guardianship) say ought to be replaced by the opposing proposition that rulership should be entrusted to a minority of persons who are specially qualified to govern by reason of their superior knowledge and virtue.[46]

Indeed, the theory of 'wilayat al-faqih', which is in embodied in the Islamic Republic of Iran, as the first actual experience of Shia political ideology, is mixed between guardianship and democracy. While the authority of the faqih and the supervision of Islamic laws and values over all political and social functions of the government emphasise the guardianship dimension of this political system, the approval of representative democracy and the participation of people in electing members of the Assembly of Experts (who choose and can remove the wilayat al-faqih'), parliament, president and many parts and local councils,

---

[45] Robert Dahl, *Democracy and its Critics*, Yale University Press, 1989, p. 55.
[46] *Ibid.*, p. 52.

show the democratic aspect of this political ideology. Article 56 of the constitution emphasizes people's sovereignty:

> *Absolute sovereignty over the word and man belongs to God, and it is He who has made man master of his own social destiny. No one can deprive man of this Divine right, nor subordinate it to the vested interests of a particular individual or group. The people are to exercise this Divine right in the manner specified in the following Article.*

This chapter aimed to clarify the conception of wilayat al-faqih and its historical background amongst Imami jurists. The next chapter will concentrate on the problem of justification and examine how the advocates of this political theory legitimize it.

Chapter Three

Why Wilayat al-Faqih?

In the previous chapter, we encountered the absolute priority of God as a fundamental component of Imami political doctrine. After all, it is He who has accorded the Holy Prophet and the Imams (peace be upon them) the authority to lead and govern the Islamic society (ummah), and 'wilayat al-faqih' is an extension of this authority. However, while the wilayat of the Imams has traditionally been verified according to Islamic theology (kalam), the guardianship of the jurists (wilayat al-faqih) is almost exclusively discussed within the sphere of jurisprudence (fiqh). Hence the universal authority of the faqih (wilayat al-amma) must be substantiated according to ijtihad (juridical reasoning). This method shall be referred to as an "internal justification" as it is intended to convince those who already accept the basic principals of the Shia creed. On the other hand, wilayat al-faqih, as a political model of guardianship, must be able to justify itself amongst other political ideologies; especially the democratic theories that essentially criticize any guardianship form of state. This approach is what we shall refer to as the "external justification" for the theory of wilayat al-faqih, and we shall return to it later.

The internal justification relies primarily on religious traditions narrated from the Holy Prophet and Imams, although some jurists also refer to rational arguments as well. Consequently, from the basis of Islamic jurisprudence, the authority of the faqih may be established according to sunnah (traditions) and reason (daleel al-aql).

Traditional Evidences for Wilayat al-Faqih

Imami jurists usually refer to a set of reports from the Prophet Muhammad and the Imams to establish wilayat al-amma for the fuqaha. We shall examine a few of them here.

A Signet Letter (Tuqih)[1] from the Absent Imam

One of the most reliable traditions adduced by scholars[2] for the purpose of this discussion is a report from the twelfth and absent Imam (May God hasten his reappearance). Shaykh al-Sadiq transmits in his book 'Ikmal al-Deen wa itmam an-Ni'ma' that Ishaq ibn Yaqub wrote a letter to the absent Imam asking him about some concerns that he had. The Imam's deputy (Muhammad ibn Uthman al-Umari) conveyed the letter to him. The Imam replied:

> As for events that may occur (al-hawadith al-waqi'a) [when you may need guidance] refer to the transmitters (ruwat) of our teachings who are my hujjah (proof) to you and I am the proof of God (Hujjatullah) to you all.[3]

---

[1] Tuqih as a word means seal and signature and in Islamic historical books and in the history of Hadith the term applies to the letters issued by Imams especially letters and decrees of the absent Imam declared through his four particular deputies.

[2] For example, Shaikh Muhammad Hassan in *Jawaher al-Kalam*, Volume 15, p. 422, Shaikh Morteza Ansari in *al-Aada wa al-Shahadat*, p. 46, Shaikh Morteza Haeri in *Salat al-Jum'a*, p. 154, Kashif al-Qeta in *al-Ferdus al-A'la*, p. 54.

[3] Shaikh al-Saduq, *Ikmal al-Din*, Ali Akbar al-Qafari (ed), Qom, 1405AH, Volume 2, Chapter 45, p. 483.

Shaykh al-Tusi also transmits the narration in the book 'al-Qayba'[4] and other collections of Imami ahadith report the tradition from the books mentioned above.

Advocates of wilayat al-faqih often refer to the second part of the tradition, namely, "they are my proof to you, and I am the proof of God to you all" to establish the authority of the fuqaha. However, some scholars (such as Imam Khomeini) maintain that the first part of the hadith may also be used to establish the authority of the faqih. The first section of this narration encourages people to ask those who relate the traditions of the Imams (peace be upon them) about any new occurrences that they encounter. It is highly unlikely that Ishaq ibn Yaqub asked the Imam about what was to be done regarding religious questions; even ordinary Shia would know that in these cases of fiqh (jurisprudence) one should refer to the fuqaha (jurists). In fact, according to some narrations, people would recourse to the students of an Imam during his lifetime. Therefore, Ishaq must have been referring to something other than this by his question about 'al-hawadith al-waqi'a', Imam Khomeini says:

> *What is meant by hawadith al-waqi'a is rather the newly arising problems that affect the people and Muslims. The question Ishaq ibn Yaqub was implicitly posing was this: now that we no longer have access to you, what should we do with respect to social problems? What is our duty?[5]*

It is necessary to establish what the Imam meant by 'ruwat' (narrators), when he commands his followers to refer to the

---

[4] Muhammad ibn Hassan al-Tusi, *Kitab al-Qayba*, Qom, 1411AH, p. 290.
[5] Imam Khomeini, *Islam and Revolution*, p. 85.

narrators of traditions with respect to these new circumstances. After all, it is self evident that people who merely transmit traditions and narrate what they have seen and heard, without a comprehensive understanding of the science of ahadith or jurisprudence, are not qualified to undertake this duty. Therefore the Imam must have been referring to the fuqaha (jurists) who are experts in the interpretation and explanation of Islamic sources.

We mentioned earlier that most Imami jurists usually refer to the second part of this tradition to establish the guardianship of the jurists. The statement makes clear that fuqaha (ruwat) act as the proof (hujjah) of the Imam in all matters in which the Imam acts as the proof of Allah. Imam Khomeini describes a 'proof of God' (or hujjah) as someone who God has designated to conduct affairs; all his deeds, actions and sayings constitute a proof for the Muslims. If the proof commands you to perform a certain act and you fail to obey him, or if despite the existence of the proof, you turn to oppressive authorities for the solution of your affairs, then God almighty will advance a proof against you on the Day of Judgment.[6]

In summary, being a hujjat implies the authority of one over his followers, and hence the injunctions of the holder of such a status must be complied with. Since the Imam as God's hujjat (the 'proof' that Allah will not accept any excuses for disobeying) has designated the fuqaha as his hujjah, the commands and directives of the fuqaha are as those of the Imam.

---

[6] *Ibid.*, p. 86.

With regards to its chain of transmission (sanad), the only issue that arises is the existence of Ishaq ibn Yaqub. There is no particular attestation of him found in the Imami books of biography (Ela al-Rejal). Hence the question may be raised, how can we be certain that the letter was really issued by the Imam and that Ibn Yaqub received the letter? There is a difference between reporting an ordinary transmission and the claim that one has received a special letter from the Imam in the era of the minor occultation, during which, access to him is only possible through his appointed deputy. The key point, however, is that many great Imami scholars such as Shaykh Sadiq, Shaykh Tusi and specially Shaykh Kolayni, who were alive during the era of the minor occultation (and were experts in ahadith) mention the tradition as 'tuqih' which is sufficient evidence for a valid chain of transmission.[7]

Maqbula of Umar ibn Hanzala

According to the science of ahadith, the 'maqbula' is a narration that has been accepted by fuqaha as a valid tradition without examining the authenticity or weakness of its chain of transmission. In other words, even though some of those who appear as its transmitters may be weak and unreliable, some evidences that support the soundness of the text compel the fuqaha to ignore such weakness.

Umar ibn Hanzala, who was a disciple of Imam as-Sadiq (pbuh) said:[8]

---

[7] Seyed Kazim Haeri, *Wilayat al-Amr fi asr al-Qayba*, Qom, Majma al-Fikr al-Islami, 1415AH, pp. 123-124.

[8] Shaikh al-Kolayni reports the tradition in *Al-Kafi*, Kitab al-Fazl al-Elm, Chapter of Ekhtelaf al-Hadith, Volume 1, p. 67 also Al-Tusi, *Tahzib al-Ahkam* , Kitab al-Qada, Volume 6, p. 218, Hadith 514.

*I asked Imam Sadiq whether it was permissible for
two of the Shia who had a disagreement concerning a
debt or an inheritance to seek the verdict of the ruler
or judge. He replied: 'anyone who has recourse to
taghut [i.e. The illegitimate ruling power], whatever
he obtains as a result of their verdict, he will have
obtained by forbidden means, even if he has a proven
right to it. For he will have obtained it through the
verdict and judgment of the taghut, the power that
almighty God has commanded him to disbelieve in.
"They wish to seek justice from illegitimate powers,
even though they have been commanded to disbelieve
therein". [Al-Qur'an, Chapter 4, Verse 60]*

Umar ibn Hanzala then asked what was the correct action for
two the Shia to take under such circumstances. Imam Sadiq
replied:

*They must seek out one of you who narrates our
traditions, who is versed in what is permissible and
what is forbidden, who is well acquainted with our
laws and ordinances, and accept him as judge and
arbiter, for I appoint him as hakim [judge].[9]*

No Imami jurist disputes that this tradition firmly establishes
the authority of a faqih with regards to the administration of
justice (wilayat al-qada). However, many leading scholars
such as Mirza al-Nayini, Sayyid Mohammad Reza
Gulpaayigani, Shaykh al-Ansari[10] and Imam Khomeini
believe that the text does not confine the authority of a faqih

---

[9] Translated in *Islam and Revolution*, p. 93.
[10] In *Kitab al-Qada wa al-Shahadat*, p. 48.

to wilayat al-qada. They assert that the Imam designated the faqih as trustees of universal authority (wilayat al-amma) when he said: "I appoint him [faqih] as hakim [judge]"

However, a judge's role is not limited to merely resolving disagreements amongst the people; their conflicts and disagreements compel them to not only recourse to judges, but also to possessors of political power. The tradition of Imam Sadiq (pbuh) unconditionally prohibits any referral to illegitimate authorities (taghut) and there is no reason to assume that the Imam solely commanded his followers not to refer to judges appointed by an illegitimate government, while allowing them to recourse to the same government for the regulation of their affairs. By appointing the faqih as hakim, the Imam made it incumbent upon all Shia to refuse any kind of recourse to illegitimate authority. Hence in all aspects of disagreement it is necessary for them to refer to a faqih, whether it is in a governmental or judicial capacity.

There are no problems surrounding this hadith's chain of transmission. All of the transmitters (Muhammad ibn Yahya, Muhammad ibn al-Hussain, Muhammad ibn Isa, Safvan ibn Yahya and Dawood ibn al-Husayn) are reliable. And although there is no specific confirmation that Umar ibn Hanzala himself existed, fuqaha generally accept this and other transmissions from him.

The Tradition of Abu Khadija

Fuqaha such as Imam Khomeini and Shaykh Muhammad Hassan[11] appeal to a famous transmission that was narrated by Abu Khadija (who was one of Imam Sadiq's

---

[11] In *Jawaher al-Kalam*, Volume 21, p. 395 and Volume 40, p. 17.

companions), to argue in favor of wilayat al-amma. The tradition is mentioned by Shaykh Tusi, Shaykh Sadiq, and Shaykh Kolayni. According to them, Abu Khadija said:

> *I was commanded by the Imam [Ja'far as-Sadiq (pbuh)] to convey the following message to our friends [Shia]: 'when enmity and dispute arise among you, or you disagree concerning the receipt or payment of a sum of money, be sure not to refer the matter to one of these malefactors for judgment. Designate as judge and arbiter someone amongst you who is acquainted with our junctions concerning what is permitted and what is prohibited, for I appoint such a man as judge over you. Let none of you take your complaint against another of you to the tyrannical ruling power.*[12]

The explanation of the argument here is similar to the previous narration. Even though the Imam says: "I appoint such a man as judge", a statement that explicitly concerns wilayat al-qada, it is essential to recognize that the final section of this transmission is not merely a repetition. Rather it is a prohibition of recourse to tyrannical authorities in matters relating to the executive. In the first instance, the Imam has commanded his followers to turn away from illegitimate judges, while in the second he has prohibited them from referring to other illegitimate powers with regard to non-judicial issues. This indicates that the appointment of a faqih is necessary in all matters of judgment and of government.

---

[12] Al-Kolayni, *Al-Foru' men al-Kafi*, Kitab al-Qada, Volume 7, p. 412; Al-Tusi, *Al-Tahzib*, Kitab al-Qada, Volume 6, p. 303; Shaikh al-Saduq, *Man la Yahzoruhu al-Faqih*, Volume 3, p. 2.

Many experts in the field of biography (Elm al-Rejal) testify that Abu Khadija is a trustworthy narrator. In addition, the hadith is well known amongst the fuqaha and classified as mashureh (famous), consequently there is no problem regarding its chain of transmission.

One might suppose that the designations issued by Imam Sadiq in the previous two traditions are temporal and limited to his lifetime. This possibility is based on the assumption that his successors may have dismissed the fuqaha from authority, just as the successors of a ruler may dismiss his previous commands. However, this supposition obviously overlooks the status of Imams within Imami Shi'ism; their commands and instructions are not equitable to those of an average ruler and their orders must be obeyed both during their lifetime and after their death. Furthermore, Imam as-Sadiq referred to a verse of the Qur'an (4:60), which ordains disbelief in taghut (oppressive authority) and prohibits any recourse to illegitimate government as a ground for his designation of the fuqaha as 'hakim'. This is a strong indication that his edict is not restricted to a specific time, and that it is forever obligatory for people to turn away from tyrannical authorities.

These three traditions are considered reliable and act as solid foundations for the establishment of wilayat al-amma. Nevertheless there are some disagreements amongst Imami jurists pertaining to the transmission and interpretation of the texts. Most critics maintain that the above-mentioned traditions confirm little more than the administration of justice (wilayat al-qada) by the fuqaha.

Aside from the three aforementioned traditions, advocates of wilayat al-amma also appeal to a set of transmissions that, although too weak to prove the universal guardianship of the faqih by themselves, certainly reinforce and verify the doctrine.

The First Tradition: The Sound Transmission of Qadah

Ali bin Ibrahim, from his father, from Hamad bin Eisa from Qadah (Abd al-Allah bin Maimun) from Imam Sadiq (pbuh), who narrated the Prophet (pbuh) as saying:

> *The superiority of the learned man over the mere worshipper is like that of the full moon over the stars. Truly the ulema (scholars) are the heirs of the Prophet (pbuh); the prophets bequeathed not gold (dinar) and silver (dirham) instead they bequeathed knowledge, and whoever acquires it has indeed acquired a generous portion of their legacy.*[13]

According to this tradition, the just and pious religious scholars (ulema) are the heirs of the Prophet; consequently, they must fulfil all the attributes and responsibilities that Allah designated for him (aside from receiving the divine revelation). Hence they are entrusted with maintaining his authority (wilayat) and the integrity of Islam. And, as has become clear from previous discussions, the Prophet has been appointed as the guardian and leader of the ummah. As the Qur'an says:

---

[13] Shaikh al-Kolayni, *Al-Kafi*, The Book of Virtue of Knowledge, Volume 1, p. 34.

The Prophet has higher claims over the believers than their own selves. [Chapter 33, Verse 6]

So his right to rule and govern over the believers is also entrusted to the scholars.

Critics believe that the tradition discusses the knowledge rather than the status of the prophets. So the scholars are the heirs of the Prophet in the field of knowledge. The hadiths' chain of transmission is sound and the fuqaha usually accept it.

The Second Tradition: Saduqs' Morsala[14].

Shaykh Saduq in several of his many books mentions the following hadith:

Imam Ali narrated the Prophet (pbuh) saying: "O God! Have mercy on those that succeed me" [Kholaphayi]. He repeated this twice and was then asked: "O Messenger of Allah, who are these that succeed you?" He replied: "They are those that come after me, transmit my traditions and practice and teach them to the people after me."[15]

The interpretation of this tradition is similar to the previous one. Those who are successors of the Prophet (pbuh) should have his status (in all areas apart from those such as receiving divine revelation), as Imam Khomeini says:

---

[14] In the study of hadith the terminology for a transmission in which the name of the first transmitter or a number of them has not been mentioned is called 'morsal'.

[15] *Uyun al-Akhbar al-Reda*, volume 2, chapter, 31, p. 37 also *Ma'ani al-Akhbar*, p. 374 also *Man la Yahzurohu al-Faqih*, Volume 4, p. 420.

To be a successor means to succeed to all the functions of Prophethood. In this respect, what is implied by the sentence, 'O God! Have mercy on my successors' is not less than what is implied by the sentence: 'Ali is my successor', since the meaning of successorship is the same in both cases.[16]

The Third Tradition: The Fuqaha are the Trustees of the Prophets

Shaykh Kolayni mentions the following hadith from the Prophet (pbuh):

The fuqaha are the trustees of the Prophets, as long as they do not concern themselves with the world (dunya). The Prophet was asked: 'what is the sign with their concern to this world?' He replied: 'By seeing whether they follow Kings (sultans). If they do that, then fear for your religion'.[17]

The argument is that the fuqaha are trustees of the Prophet not merely with respect to deducing Islamic laws, but with all the duties and functions of the Prophet (pbuh) and this encompasses the establishment of a religious government and a just social system.

The Fourth Tradition: The Ulema are the Rulers

Amody transmits a tradition from the Commander of the faithful, Ali (pbuh):

---

[16] Imam Khomeini, *Islam and Revolution*, p. 72.
[17] Kolayni, *al-Kafi*, Volume 1, p. 46.

The ulema [scholars] are the rulers [hakim] over people.[18]

The meaning of this tradition explicitly supports wilayat al-amma, but the chain of transmission is weak.

The Fifth Tradition: Imam Hussain's Sermon

During a sermon about enjoining good and forbidding evil, Imam Hussein (pbuh) addressed the scholars and said:

...The disaster that has befallen you is greater than what has befallen others, for the true rank and degree ulema has been taken away from you. The administration of the country and the issuing of orders should actually be entrusted to religious scholars (ulema) who are guardians of the rights of God and knowledgeable about Gods ordinances concerning what is permitted and what is forbidden. But your position has been usurped from you, for no other reason than you have abandoned the pivot of truth and have disagreed about the nature of the sunnah, despite the existence of clear proofs. If you were strong in the face of torturing and suffering and prepared to endure hardship for God's sake, then all proposed regulations would be brought to you for your approval and for you to issue.[19]

If it were not for the weakness of its chain of transmission, the tradition would have been the most explicit verification wilayat al-amma.

---

[18] Amodi, *Qorar al-Hekam*, Volume 1, p. 137, 506.

[19] Harrani ibn Shobeh, *Tohaf al-Uqul*, Qom, 1404AH, Volume 1, p. 238.

The Sixth Tradition: The Fuqaha are the Fortress of Islam

Shaykh Kolayni mentions the tradition from Imam Kazim (pbuh):

> *Believers who are fuqaha are the fortresses of Islam, like the encircling walls that protect a city.*[20]

The statement, which is that the fuqaha are the fortresses of Islam, means that fuqaha have a duty to protect Islam. They must do whatever is necessary to fulfil that duty hence they need to follow the Prophet as a good example for every believer. The Qur'an says:

> *Certainly there is for you in them a good example, for him who fears Allah and the last day.* [Chapter 60, Verse 6]

The Prophet (pbuh) as the fortress of Islam did not restrict himself for training and teaching to protect Islam, rather he undertook socio-political duties and functions as well, hence all the tasks entrusted to the Prophet Muhammad must also be fulfilled by the well qualified fuqaha, as a matter of duty to become the true fortresses of Islam.

Wilayat al-Amma as Hisbah

By referring to textual evidences (the Qur'an and ahadith), advocates of universal authority (wilayat al-amma) intend to illustrate that well qualified fuqaha not only have priority over others to govern the believers, but are also explicitly designated as guardians (wali) of the Muslim community. However, some Imami jurists maintain that even when you

---

[20] Al-Kolayni, *Al-Kafi*, Volume 1, p. 38.

overlook the traditional proofs of wilayat al-faqih, one can establish the same authority for the faqih by considering 'hisbah'. Although this method of reasoning cannot confirm the designation of the faqih as wali, it does emphasize the priority of the fuqaha to undertake these social duties and makes clear that their authority is legitimate.

'Hisbah' as a word literally means reward or spiritual wage, and it is usually applied to deeds that are done to please God and seek heavenly reward (thawab). In Islamic jurisprudence, this term refers to something that God is not willing to ignore or overlook. For instance, there are people who are minors or suffer from insanity, who are unable to discharge their own affairs and need someone to take care of them. If they have no father or grandfather, someone else should undertake their responsibilities and since these who prepare themselves to be in charge of their affairs do that for the sake of God, it is called 'hisbah'.

There is an important difference between 'hisbah' and what is referred to as sufficient necessity (wajib al-kefai). Sufficient necessity is an obligation that everyone one can fulfil, but if undertaken by a sufficient number of individuals, other people are relieved of their duty, whereas 'hisbah' should be undertaken by the faqih. If a qualified jurist is not available, then only the just believers (mumineen adil) have the right to be in charge of such affairs.

Having clarified the meaning of 'hisbah', we will now examine an argument that presupposes the extension of its denotation. People who adopt this line of reasoning argue that 'hisbah' is not restricted to its traditional examples such as in the case of minors and the insane. Rather, the philosophy and reasoning behind such a role demand its extension to social and political affairs. This argument has two major premises:

Muslims are obliged to observe the instructions and prohibitions of Islam in all areas of their personal and social lives, and some of these realistically require the authority and apparatus of a state in order to be practically implemented. Furthermore, it is impermissible for the believers to allow illegitimate and unjust rulers to govern their society, while they have the potential to manage their own affairs independently. From a juridical perspective, this premise is universally accepted.

A just faqih must undertake the duty of social and political guardianship for two reasons: either that the traditional evidences supporting wilayat al-amma are sound, or the just faqih has priority over others to undertake this duty. The reason behind this is that no one has the right to establish his authority over another unless they are qualified to undertake the duty of 'hisbah' (guardianship). And the protection of Islam and Islamic society is an instance of 'hisbah', which means God is not willing to ignore or overlook it, consequently well-qualified fuqaha have priority over ordinary people to bear this responsibility. In other words, necessarily someone has to undertake the function. We have two options; either to delegate the authority to those who have no professional knowledge about Islam or approve the authority of a just faqih. We have natural misgivings about the former when the later is feasible. Therefore, the fuqaha have a duty and a right to fulfil it.[21]

---

[21] Seyed Kazim Haeri, *Wilayat al-Amr fi Asr al-Qayba*, p. 96.

Despite the traditional arguments illustrating that the fuqaha have been designated as wali, this argument merely establishes the priority of a faqih to be in charge of governmental affairs similar to other cases of hisbah.

The Rational Argument

Recourse to rational argument has a long history amongst Shia scholars. Some believe that the rational theory was first adopted by the Zaydi Shia, al-Qasim ibn Ibrahim (785 - Medina 860), who argued that divinely appointed political authority is necessary due to the imperfections of human nature.[22] Mullah Ahmad Naraqi (d. 1829), the author of 'Avaed al-Ayyam', was the first Imami jurist who appealed to logical reasoning to support the concept of universal authority (wilayat al-amma).

This approach adopts a similar structure to those rational arguments upon which Shia scholars base the necessity of Prophethood and Imamate; that it was necessary for God to appoint some people as Prophets and Imams in order to provide divine guidance to mankind. Therefore it is only reasonable to assume that in the absence of such infallible guidance, God would entrust the responsibilities of religious and political leadership to those people best qualified to undertake it as deputies of the absent, infallible Imam.

Two strands of argument are presented as a justification of wilayat al-faqih. The first of which is an argument consisting entirely of rational premises without reference to the Qur'an or traditions, while the second is an argument established by a combination of reasoning and textual evidences. However,

---

[22] Antony Black, *The History of Islamic Political Thought*, p. 40.

purely rational arguments are generally unable to definitively establish the prophecy or leadership of a particular person. Rational arguments must typically consist of universal, certain and necessary premises, and consequently, pure reasoning can prove the necessity of Prophethood and Imamate, although these rational arguments often encompass an explanation of qualifications that the ideal leader should have (e.g. sinless or just). Although there are many different lines of reasoning, it will suffice here to mention a few of them. In his volume concerning theology, Avecina (Ibn Sina) presents a discussion based on the necessity of a well-organised social order in order to establish the necessity of prophets.[23] Although this argument has naturally been appealed to by Muslim scholars and philosophers in order to establish and define Prophethood, the addition of some premises gives it the potential to confirm the necessity of its continuation in the vicegerency of the fuqaha. The structure of modified version of the proof is as follows:

1. Man is a social being and therefore necessarily needs social order to overcome many of his conflicts and affairs.

2. Human social life and order should be designed so that it provides individual social happiness.

3. A set of adequate and perfect laws and the existence of one who is capable of executing these laws and leading society are two necessary conditions for the establishment of an ideal society.

---

[23] Ibn Sina, *Al-Shefa,* The book of Al-Elahiyat, The 10th Article, Chapter 2, p. 487.

4. It is not in the power of human beings to establish an ideal, just, and truly well-ordered society without the aid of God and His divine laws.

5. To avoid any deficiency, interference or possession of God's message (revelation), the Prophets who delivers His message must be infallible.

6. The explanation of the contents of the perfect religion and the execution of its laws prerequisite the appointment of infallible Imams.

7. When there is no access to infallible Imams for attaining the above-mentioned aim (3), the leaders who are just and are expert in religious knowledge (Just faqih).[24]

The first four premises prove the necessity of prophecy and that it is necessary for God to send prophets. The sixth one extends the reasoning to the question of Imamate and the necessity of an infallible Imam. And the final premise establishes the necessity of a qualified religious leader in the era of the absent Imam.

Another rational argument has been presented by Ayatollah Borujerdi who applied some historical and religious premises in his reasoning.

1. The leader and ruler of a society must be entrusted with the protection of social order and meet the essential needs of the people.

2. Islam has paid attention to those essential needs and has legislated suitable laws. The ruler (wali) of Islamic society is responsible for the execution of these laws.

---

[24] Abdullah Javadi Amoli, *Wilayat ul-Faqih*, Qom: Esra Publication, 1378AH, pp. 151-152.

3. Within the early period of Islam, the Prophet (pbuh) and the Imams (pbut) were the legitimate political leaders and the organisation of political and social affairs was their duty.

4. The need to regulate social relationships according to divine laws and values is not confined to a specific period of time. Rather it is a crucial need for every age and generation. Certainly when infallible Imams were present amongst people, they appointed reliable people as their representatives to undertake Shia social affairs and prevent their followers from recourse to tyrannical governments (taghut) for their affairs. The assumption that Imams encouraged people to avoid referring to taghut without presenting an alternative solution to their problems is illogical.

Considering the previous premise, it is also logical that just fuqaha should be appointed as their representatives and deputies in the era of greater absence because there are only three possibilities:

*   A non-faqih (one who is not a just faqih) is designated as the Imam's deputy. This supposition is obviously unwise and impractical, as a person lacking the essential knowledge or qualifications would be unable to provide guidance.
*   In the era of occultation, Imami have a duty to avoid any recourse to illegitimate government for their social affairs, however the Imams did not introduce any alternative point of reference. This theory is equally impractical.

- The Imam has designated the just faqih as his deputy to undertake these affairs and that is what we are seeking.[25]

Before concluding the internal justifications of wilayat al-faqih, it is necessary for the sake of our discussion to examine what qualifications a deputy of the Imam must have. Although we have previously mentioned that only a well-qualified jurist may be considered the Imam's deputy (neyab), we have not yet discussed what qualifications he requires according to Islamic sources, i.e. Qur'an and Sunnah.

The Characteristics of Wali al-Faqih and the Problem of 'A'lamiya'

When compared to other political doctrines, Imami political thought has some significant advantages. For example, when it insists that the ruler of the society must possess specific characteristics. In modern democratic systems, factors such as popularity, being telegenic and having the support of a powerful party and large corporations are the most important factors, while individual virtues and qualifications are often neglected. Shia political thought, on the other hand, makes the personal characteristics of a political leader an essential factor. Some of these are as follows.

Ijtihad (Proficiency in Islamic Jurisprudence)

Since the implementation of Islamic laws and values in the various aspects of social life are one of the most important aims of an Islamic state, the ruler must naturally have expertise and knowledge in Islamic thought in order to be

---

[25] Hussain Borujerdi, *Al-Badr al-Zaher fi Salat ul-Jom'a wal-Mosafer*, Qom, 1367AH, pp. 72-78.

able to make socio-political decisions and issue orders according to the Islamic point of view. Many traditional proofs of wilayat al-amma insist that the wali (hakim) must be a faqih:

In maqbula of Umar ibn Hanzala, Imam Sadiq (pbuh) says:

> *They must seek out one of you who narrates our traditions, who is versed in what is permissible and what is forbidden, who is well acquainted with our laws and ordinance, and accept him as judge and arbiter, for I appoint him as hakim.*[26]

In the tradition of Abu Khadija too, Imam says:

> *Designate as judge and arbiter someone among you who is acquainted with our injunctions concerning what is permitted and prohibited.*[27]

In a signed letter the Absent Imam (may Allah hasten his reappearance) writes:

> *As for events that may occur, refer to the transmitters of our teachings.*[28]

As we have already discussed, these titles and attributes correspond with a just and competent faqih's (mujtahid) abilities, and not those who merely transmit traditions.

---

[26] Muhammad Hassan Hor al-A'meli, *Wasael al-Shi'a*, Qom: Ahl ul-Bait Institution, 1412AH, Volume 27, p. 137.

[27] *Al-Kafi*, Volume 7, p. 412.

[28] Shaikh al-Saduq, *Ikmal al-Din*, Volume 2, p. 483.

Justice

Justice is a quality required of all forms of authority and leadership in Imami political doctrine; judges and prayer leaders must all be considered fair and capable, and their roles are considerably less than those who rule an entire state. In addition, the Qur'an teaches Muslims to have no inclination and cooperation with unjust people and tyrannical authorities:

> *And do not incline to those who are unjust, lest the fire shall touch you, and you have no guardians beside Allah, then shall you not be helped. [Chapter 11, Verse 113]*

In some verses of the Qur'an Allah Almighty invites the believers to show their disobedience to unjust people, those who commit great sins:

> *And do not obey the bidding of the extravagant, (those) who make mischief in the land and do not act right.* [Chapter 26, Verses 151-152]

> *Do not follow him whose heart we have made unmindful to our remembrance and he follows his low desires and his case is one in which due bounds are exceeded.* [Chapter 18, Verse 28]

Although justice has not been stipulated in the traditional proofs of wilayat al-faqih examined in the course of this subject, the Qur'an and a number of transmissions criticize unjust rulers and those who are obedient to tyrannical governors. They also maintain that a community founded on Islamic laws and teachings, cannot be run by someone who does not believe in or behave in accordance to justice. To cite an example, Imam Muhammad al-Baqir (A) said to Muhammad b. Muslim:

> *O Muhammad, surely the unjust rulers and those who follow them are separated from God's religion. Certainly they went astray, and led many astray.*[29]

Prudence, Trustworthiness, Administrative Facilities, and Courage

Such qualities are obvious requirements of any appropriate political leader, thus there is no need to mention evidences regarding them.

Knowledge

Many evidences stipulate that a trustee of Islamic political authority must be amongst the most knowledgeable ('alem), competent and qualified of Islamic scholars. This criterion is somewhat contentious however, as many of the traditions mentioned in it's support have weak chains of transmission.

According to the book of Solaim b. Qais, Ali (p) says:

> *Does anyone deserve to be the ruler (caliph) over the ummah except one who is most knowledgeable of God's book (Qur'an) and the Prophet (pbuh)'s traditions (sunnah). Allah says in the Qur'an (10:35), "Is he then, who guides to the truth, more worthy to*

---

[29] *Al-Kafi*, Volume 1, p. 184.

be followed, or he who himself does not go aright unless he is guided? "[30]

It is transmitted from the Prophet (pbuh) that he said:

One who leads his people, while there are among them more knowledgeable than he, their sovereignty (the people's) would begin to decline forever.[31]

As we mentioned in the previous chapter, a just faqih has various functions. Some of them like the administration of justice (qada) and 'hisbah' are categorized as 'wilayat', whilst others such as 'ifta' do not require a designation from the Imam. In the context of the present subject, it is essential to determine which of these functions is dependant on 'alamiyat' (being the most knowledgeable).

Reference to Imami jurists' decrees shows that those who consider 'alamiyat as a condition have merely concentrated on 'ifta'. Ayatollah Sayyid Kazim Yazdi, the author of 'al-'urwat ul-wuthqa' writes:

With regard to a mujtahid's functions, none of them are restricted by al-'alamiya but taqleed (ifta). The matter of his wilayat however, is not conditioned by al-'alamiya.[32]

Many great Imami jurists who have commented upon this important book (al-urwat ul-wuthqa), such as Ayatollahs

---

[30] Solaim ibn Qais Al-Helali, *Kitab al-Solaim*, Tehran: Dar al-Kotob al-Islamiya, p. 118.
[31] Barqi, *Al-Mahasin*, Volume 1, p. 93.
[32] *Al-Urvat ul-Wosqa*, The Chapter of Ijtihad wal-Taqlid, Question 68.

Haery, Mirza al-Nayini, Aqa Ziya al-Araki, Sayyid Abul-Hassan al-Esfahani, Burujerdi, Khomeini, Khui, Milani, and Gulpaayigani, do not add any marginal notes to this decree of Yazdi, which means they agree with him that the functions of the faqih that exercises his authority (wilayat) are not conditioned by being the most knowledgeable.

Shaykh al-Ansari also maintains that 'alamiya is not necessary in the designation of a faqih as wali (hakim)'. Every just faqih has the right to undertake affairs which require justified authority (wilayat). He believes that only when fuqaha have different decrees (fatwa) the decree of the one who is most knowledgeable ('alam) has priority over others.[33]

Shaykh Muhammad Hassan, the author of 'Jawahir al-Kalam', also believes that the traditional proofs, which state that the fuqaha are designated as 'wali' and the deputies of the Imam, emphasize on the professional knowledge about Islam (fiqahat) and not upon the 'most knowledgeable' as the condition of a faqih's wilayat.[34]

Essentially with regards to some functions of the faqih such as 'qada', it seems incredible if one supposes that it is conditioned on 'alamiya because this implies on a very large scale that the Shia community has only one faqih who has legitimate authority to judge.

Finally, we have indicated that 'Ijtihad' has various aspects and therefore it is quite reasonable to assume 'X' is the most

---

[33] Shaikh al-Ansari, *Taqlid*, Published by International Congress of Shaikh al-Ansari publications, p. 67.

[34] *Jawahir al-Kalam*, Volume 40, pp. 44-45

knowledgeable (a'lem) in chapters of Islamic jurisprudence concerning worship (such as praying and fasting), while 'Y' is a'lem in the chapters of transactions (moamelat) and 'Z' is the most knowledgeable in the context of the administration of justice and punishment (hudud). Consequently, we have to take into account the relationship between a function that a faqih wants to undertake and the kind of knowledge that is a prerequisite to that function. There is no sufficient reason to convince us that one who is the most knowledgeable in chapters of worship would be able to perform the function of 'qada' better than a faqih who is most knowledgeable in administration of justice.

On the other hand, ijtihad and fiqahat are but one characteristic that a leader of the Islamic society should have. There is no reason to concentrate on the priority of 'a'lem' and thereby ignore other qualifications that walis (fuqaha) must possess, which might provide them with the necessary abilities and characteristics of a ruler. Certainly, in a situation wherein a few faqih are completely equal in all qualifications of leadership except ijtihad, one might claim that the authority of a'lem has priority over others, especially when he is the most knowledgeable in social-political aspects of Islamic law. But it should be noted that even this is merely a 'rational preference', because as the author of Jawaher al-Kalam indicated, the traditional proofs of wilayat al-faqih are silent about alamiya as a condition of wilayat.

The External Justification

Many political theories are known as 'guardianship' in spite of the profound differences they have with one another. By guardianship, we mean a political system in which the state is governed by qualified rulers (guardians). The ruler or rulers are not subject to election and do not come to office through free election. They deserve to govern the people due to their specific qualifications and abilities. Therefore, the delegation of authority in a guardianship model of state is not due to a democratic process, but rather to the qualities of a guardian. Advocates of guardianship commonly believe that the entrustment of political power to a highly qualified minority, who has exceptional expertise, guarantees the interests and good of the people. Although the followers of guardianship disagree about the qualifications the guardians must have, or about the interpretation of happiness and people's good. This is why the guardianship supported by Plato is rationally different from the Marxist Leninist interpretation of it. Plato's guardians are a minority of well-qualified philosophers, whereas the latter's are an organized group of revolutionaries.

There are many arguments to justify guardianship over democracy. Although on the other hand, guardianship in turn faces many criticisms, especially from advocates of democracy. So if we admit that 'wilayat al-faqih' is a political doctrine belonging to the guardianship model of state, it must be able to overcome its critics and eventually establish itself as a reasonable, rational and legitimate political doctrine. That is what is meant by 'external justification', which, contrary to 'internal justification', does not rely on religiously accepted reasoning.

First of all, we must assess why and how 'wilayat al-faqih' poses as a guardianship regime. According to this theory of state, a just, capable and pious jurist, who possesses a number of qualities, has legitimate authority to govern the society in the era of occultation (ghaibat). This obviously indicates that other kinds of experts and average people have no equal access to the highest political office and only specific experts (jurists) have the right and the opportunity to attain the highest level of political leadership. Moreover, they are not elected by people, but are instead designated by Imams as 'wali' and possessors of the authority.

On the other hand, the unique example of this political system, whose detailed blueprints are embedded in the constitution of the Islamic republic of Iran, does not adopt a pure system of guardianship. After all, it's constitution respects a limited democratic processes in that the majority of governmental institutions, even the political leadership is chosen through elections. According to article 107, a group of elected experts (a few jurists are elected by people every seven years) shall elect a well-qualified faqih as the political leader. Both the authority of shari'a (wilayat al-faqih) and the sovereignty of the people in this political regime make it a mixture of democracy and guardianship. Hence it should be categorized as a 'meritocracy', because it does not go hand in hand with all the standards of guardianship. What distinguishes this model of 'meritocracy' from guardianship is the role of the people in participating in the distribution of political power and in shaping political decisions through their representatives. However, people and their representatives are not religiously free to delegate the political authority to a non-faqih or those who have no tendency to rule, legislate and execute within the framework of divine laws and Islamic values and teachings. Consequently, in this meritocracy, a just Imami jurist as 'wilayat al-faqih' and a group of fuqaha as the 'guardian council', supervise and control the decisions and functions of representatives and bureaucrats, who are themselves subject to the democratic process. The central discussion here concerns the relationship between 'wilayat al-faqih' and what traditionally are stated as the foundation and justification of the guardianship. We must now evaluate whether these foundations are adequate to cite as justifications of 'wilayat al-faqih' and how could this doctrine overcome the critiques of guardianship.

Some advocates of guardianship hold that ordinary people lack the necessary qualifications for ruling. They seem to lack much understanding of their own basic needs, interests and good. Many of them are unable or unwilling to do whatever may be necessary to attain deep knowledge about their own needs and good as well as the appropriate means to achieve these needs and goods. In conclusion, people have no political competence to govern themselves. Their deficiency is partly in knowledge, partly in virtue i.e. strong tendencies to seek good ends; hence they are not qualified to govern. This approach undermines the fundamental ground of democracy and supports the idea that guardians who have sufficient political competence should govern people.

Obviously, the doctrine of 'wilayat al-faqih' does not rely on the political incompetence of people to justify the priority of the faqih's authority. Neither in traditional proofs of 'wilayat al-faqih' nor in the rational ones, do Imami scholars stress on people's deficiencies. Some rational proofs of 'wilayat al-faqih' depend on the belief that it is not in the power of human beings to establish an ideal, ordered society with no aid of God's revelation. Clearly, this premise expresses the deficiency of human beings as such, and not simply the imperfection of ordinary people, confirming the competence of a small minority as guardians. Indeed, this deficiency justifies man's need of religion, and its important role in organizing social relationships.

The second foundation mentioned as a reason for guardianship consists of a specific conception of governing. For them, ruling people is an art. Therefore, rulers must be experts of a certain type, meaning experts in the art of governing. They as guardians would be specialists whose specialization would make them superior in the art of leadership, not only in comparison with ordinary people but also with other kinds of experts such as economists, physicists, engineers and so on. Although most people are potentially capable of acquiring the qualifications needed for leadership, they lack the time to acquire them. A society needs many different types of experts. The need for acquiring different skills and then implementing them, makes it impossible for each and every person to spend the time they would need to gain the moral and instrumental competence for ruling. To suppose that a large number of people each have the capacity to acquire and use numerous specialized skills is not realistic. Consequently, in a well ordered society some persons should be rigorously trained and selected to function well as rulers (guardians). Because leadership is so crucial nothing could be of greater importance than the education of our rulers.[35]

Apart from the fact that many scholars have misgivings about the actual existence of the art of governing, this argument exclusively supports the Platonic version of guardianship. There is no single art or science that can provide us with the moral and technical knowledge and

---

[35] *Democracy and its Critics*, pp. 62-63.

abilities required for being an ideal leader. Many versions of guardianship, including 'wilayat al-faqih', do not look at guardians as specialists in the art of governing. Instead, they believe that the duty of governing should delegate to a few qualified persons, because of some certain qualifications and abilities that they have. Guardians have a advantage over others in matters of leadership, such as their in depth knowledge of ideological, great commitment to the ambitions of specific party, being vanguard and leader in revolution or possession the knowledge that is necessary for shaping particular social formation.

The unique reason that justifies (apart from traditional religious reasons) the ruling of the fuqaha as guardians, pertains to their knowledge about Shari'a which must be accompanied with personal virtues and moral competence. It is true that moral competence is not confined to a small minority and that many people have the capacity to gain moral competence and become just and pious. However, what distinguishes the just fuqaha and render them the unique group who has legitimate authority to rule over the believers is their expertise in Islamic jurisprudence. The justification of the guardianship of fuqaha is owed to the fundamental role of Islamic law in the lives of Muslims. Islam obliges Muslims to adopt Islamic laws and values in both their individual as well as public lives. Consequently, one who has the ability (as a jurisprudent) that is necessary for undertaking this task must be in charge of ruling the people. Therefore, the question of 'wilayat al-faqih' is not a question of having a specific art. It has roots in a religious belief that sees a crucial role for shari'a in Islamic society.

The distinction between the general good and personal interests could provide the advocates of guardianship the third reason for justification. The case of guardianship sometimes rest on assumption that the composition of the general good (general interest) and how the knowledge of what composes the general good may be acquired. If the general good were only composed of individual interests and if we were to believe that everyone could pursue his personal interests without guardians, then the guardianship model of state would be unnecessary and undesirable. But if the general good and interest of society consists of something more than an aggregation of personal interests, then to achieve it will require more than this. To bring about the general good would then require an understanding of the ways in which the general good differs from a combination individual interests. If it is also true that most people are mainly concerned with their own individual interests instead of that of the general public, then the task of deciding on the general good should be entrusted to those especially trained to understand what the general good consists of. Obviously, that depends on what is meant by the general good.[36]

Although the followers of 'wilayat al-faqih' do not fully accept this argument, however, a modified version of it would sufficiently justify this model of guardianship. Islam as a perfect religion aims for real human happiness, hence, its laws and teachings are necessarily established for the ultimate self-realization of the human being and for gaining true salvation. From this point of view both the good of the individual as well as the general public are harmonized with the contents of Islam. Concepts such as public interest should not be defined without considering of the crucial role

---

[36] *Ibid.*, pp. 70-71.

played by Islam in both the public and private spheres. When one acknowledges this fact, which is especially true in a society where most people believe that Islam is the ultimate way to salvation, the following argument could be supposed as external justification for the doctrine of 'Willayat al-faqih':

1. General interest and public good are not merely a composition of individual interests and they must be determined through a higher source.

2. Within an Islamic society the real public good and interest cannot be known while neglecting Islamic laws and values. It does not mean that other kinds of expertise play no role in the process of determining public good, rather, the key point is that all political and economic decisions, various legislations as well as government orders must take Islamic teachings (especially jurisprudence) seriously and harmonize themselves with the demands of Islam.

3. People are mostly concerned with their own individual interests so the task of deciding the public interest, at least in cases that are specifically dealt with by Islam should not be entrusted to the ups and downs of public opinion.

4. Technocrats and those who are experts in the various sciences are often more concerned than average people with the good and interest of the public. However, as mentioned in the second premise, in an Islamic society technocrats as policymakers can not have a full understand of the public good, unless they are experts in Islamic thought.

Policymaking, legislation, organizing the system of rights and duties and other significant functions of government must be done under the supervision and authority of a well qualified faqih (or fuqaha) who is just, brave, honest, intelligent, knowledgeable about social and political issues, and an expert in Islamic ideology.

This external justification seems quite convincing within a specific context, that is, for those who pursue Islamic culture and support the establishment of an Islamic society. For those who do not believe in Islam, the premises of this justification (particularly the second and fourth) need further evidence.

Criticism of Guardianship

Advocates of democracy usually criticize guardianship and its justifications. We have to consider briefly a few of these criticisms to assess how the connection between the doctrine of wilayat al-faqih and these critiques might be? In my view the three following criticisms are more significant than the others:

i)   Adversaries of guardianship insist that the keystone of this theory that tries to justify the deserts of guardians to rule based on their knowledge is disputable. The possession of this religious knowledge is not sufficient enough to prove that political power should be entrusted to a faqih to protect and promote public welfare and prosperity. How can we know that the guardian is not seeking his own interests rather than that of the general public? Is there any system of control over them to prevent hem from abusing his authority? In the guardianship model of state, since the people do not delegate authority to the guardian, they cannot legally or constitutionally withdraw political power from the guardian. The guardians are free of popular controls.

ii) Unlike democracy that provides people with the opportunity to engage in governing themselves and to improve their moral-political experiences, the guardianship system of rule prevents an entire population from developing their social, political and moral capacities. This is essentially because only a few people (guardians) are engaging in governing. Therefore, only a few people have the opportunity to learn how to act as morally responsible human beings. Only guardians can exercise the freedom of participating in the process of making laws, while in democratic states the whole population enjoys that freedom. Even though in many democratic states, the cooperate and political elite are far more powerful than ordinary citizens, however, they cannot be compared to guardians. These elites are not despots and people can still play a role in the distribution of political power and in making political decisions.

iii) Guardianship is based upon the idea that there is a set of truths, objective propositions and valid knowledge that can determine public good or true social interests. The second pillar of guardianship rests on the point that only those who have this knowledge[37] (what does public good

---

[37] There is no agreement among advocates of guardianship about the nature of this knowledge therefore they disagree about the qualifications of this small minority of rulers (guardians). For instance, in the eyes of Plato this knowledge consists of a set of propositions about what is best for the community. This knowledge is based on rational certainty that ordinary people have no access to. Unlike true philosophers, ordinary people just have opinions (uncertainties) instead of knowledge (rational certainty).

consist of and by what means can we achieve it?) are exclusively competent to hold political authority. Some critics of guardianship criticize the first pillar of the argument. They emphasize that there is no such thing as rational, unquestionable, or objective knowledge. There are no determined truths as 'science of ruling' that can justify the authority of a few people as guardians. In addition, they believe advocates of guardianship face the problem of validation because they can not establish why their understanding of public good and social interests is objectively true. Robert Dahl writes:

In judging the validity of statements about the general good we can and should employ reason and experience. Nonetheless, no assertion that 'the public good definitely consists of such and such' can be shown to be 'objectively true' in the same sense that many statements in mathematics, logic, or the natural sciences are understood to be objectively true.[38]

To clarify the relationship between these critiques and the Imami political doctrine of wilayat al-faqih we have to keep in mind that these criticisms are targeting 'pure guardianship', a political theory that leaves no room for people in political affairs while entrusting complete political

---

From an entirely different perspective, Marxist-Leninists maintain that this knowledge consists of the laws of historical development based on 'historical materialism' as a rigorous methodological approach rooted in the belief that the structure of society and human relations in all their forms are the product of material conditions and circumstances rather than of ideas, thought or consciousness. Consequently, for them the guardians are a few revolutionaries who know the laws and material conditions that rule over these historical developments.

[38] *Democracy and its Critics*, p. 71.

authority to non-elected minority (guardians). In the next chapter it will be explained that wilayat al-faqih is compatible with a specific version of democracy called 'religious democracy'. In any case the mixture between the authority of a just faqih who represents both the authority of Islamic jurisprudence as well as the authority of the people, renders some of these criticisms essentially irrelevant to the doctrine of wilayat al-faqih. For example the second critique mentioned above is absolutely inapplicable to the guardianship of the faqih. Moreover, according to what has been discussed in the previous chapter about the meaning of absolute authority of a just faqih, the first criticism is also irrelevant, because the guardianship of a faqih is not beyond the control of a group of elected experts who supervise and control his usage of power and authority. In addition, it is the religious responsibility of all Muslims to be not neutral about the behavior of their governors and leaders.

In the previous pages it is clear that the guardianship of the faqih is not base on the assumption that leadership is a specific art or knowledge that consists of a set of truths and skills. Therefore, the final criticism cannot undermine this version of guardianship either. Almost all Shi'a scholars believe in rationalism, hence, the problem of validation is very important in their eyes. This is true not only with regards to fundamental Islamic beliefs, but also in other aspects of Islamic thought including political thought. They attempt to justify their system of beliefs through rational arguments, as well as through traditional evidences. As a result, Shi'a political thought is based upon a set of true, valid and objective doctrines about human nature, the philosophy of life, and morality. It consists of a set of philosophical-theological statements that produce an Islamic world's view. Indeed, this theory of state like other political theories is rested upon a comprehensive philosophy and the justification of this political thought is due to the justification of its moral-philosophical foundations as well. However, we do not believe in 'hard rationalism', which demands that all religious statements and beliefs must be verified by decisive rational proofs, exactly as with mathematics. Obviously, religious statements and beliefs should be categorized according to their own appropriate methods of justification. Islam consists of objective truths and valid statements; however, one can not prove its validation by recourse to a unique methodology (rational proofs). Unlike the fundamental doctrines of Islam (usul al-Din) that can largely be validated and justified through rational arguments, the validation of Islamic law is, to a large extent, based upon trust in the commands of God, which in turn can be established by appealing to rational proof.

The key point is that the validity of this model of guardianship (wilayat al-faqih) does not acquire its approbation from the assumption that there is an objective art or science for ruling people or a specific knowledge used for understanding public good and finding the means for achieving them. Its verification is due to the validation of Islam's moral, philosophical and theological foundations including the importance of Shari'a for our ultimate happiness.

The external justification of wilayat al-faqih consists of two independent sides, the positive and the negative. Positive justification aims to justify the validation of this theory directly and through the emphasis on the necessity of the

Islamic legal system and the implementation of its laws for the establishment of an ideal social and personal existence. However, the negative side refers to any efforts undertaken to prove the priority of this doctrine over its alternatives. Since the doctrine of democracy in general and the theory of liberal democracy in particular is the most important alternative theory facing guardianship, the external justification of our political theory would be insufficient if we fail to assess the relationship between the theory of wilayat al-faqih and democracy. The next chapter will attempt to make complete the external justification of this political doctrine by evaluating the nature of democracy and its possible connections to this version of guardianship.

There is another significant reason why we should discuss democracy. Some Muslim thinkers maintain that Islam fundamentally disagrees with democracy. Hence, in their eyes our interpretation of imami political thought that mixes the guardianship of the faqih with elements of democracy is totally wrong and is against the foundations of Islam.

Chapter Four

Islam and Democracy

Contemporary Islamic political thought has become deeply influenced by attempts at reconciling Islam and democracy. Muslim thinkers who deal with political debates cannot ignore the significance of the democratic system, as it is the prevailing theme of modern western political thought. Thus it is necessary for any alternative political system, whether it is religious or secular, to explore its position with regards to democratic government. In the past, prominent Islamic thinkers such as Imam Khomeini, Mirza Muhammad Hussain Nayini and al-Kawakibi maintained that a democratic Islamic form of government is a compatible and practical thesis, believing that a constitution could protect and guarantee both the essential Islamic as well as democratic aspects of government.

In contrast to this more optimistic approach, many fundamentalist thinkers argue that Islam and democracy are irreconcilably opposed, and that there exists a clear contradiction between Islamic and democratic principles. This opinion has emerged as a result of their perception of the source from which democracy came, the creed from which it emanated, the basis upon which it has been established as well as the ideas and systems of thought with which it is currently associated. However, opposition to religious democracy is not confined to fundamentalists; advocates of a secular state also believe that the concept of a democratic Islamic government is a paradoxical thesis, and they often refer to a selection of Islamic rulings and beliefs that they construe as antagonistic to the foundations and underlying values of the democratic system.

Other Muslim intellectuals maintain that any apparent incompatibility or conflict between the ideas of religion and democracy are caused by the misinterpretation of Islam. They maintain that there is no conflict between democracy and an understanding of religion, which is changing, rational and in harmony with accepted extra-religious criteria and values. They believe that by reinterpreting Islam and constantly reviewing and renewing its beliefs, the vision of a religious democracy would be completely feasible and indeed desirable.

Consequently the question of whether or not religious democracy is feasible has given rise to four major schools of thought amongst thinkers and Muslim political movements:

1. The implementation of Islamic laws (shari'a) and the establishment of an Islamic society based upon Islamic values is possible within a constitutionally Islamic and democratic political system. The participation of citizens in making political decisions can serve the socio-political aims of Islam and democracy merely acts as a system and method for the distribution of political power and a means by which citizens express their opinions.

2. There is an obvious conflict between the traditional juridical (fiqhi) based conception of Islam and democracy. The establishment of a religious democratic government is in need of a rethinking, reinterpretation and review of Islamic thought in order for it to become harmonious with contemporary global and philosophical

foundations, values and implications of democracy. Therefore, the practicality of religious democracy rests upon the reformation of traditional religious knowledge.

3. Democracy is a system of disbelief (kufr) and is totally and completely irreconcilable with Islamic beliefs and principles. Commitment to Islam leaves no room for democracy.

4. The fourth approach arrives at the same conclusion as the third, that the idea of a democratic Islamic government is paradoxical. However, unlike advocates of the third approach, this group emphasizes the desirability and justification of democracy, and insists that religion cannot possibly satisfy the values and foundations that democracy requires.

These approaches shall be addressed in detail later in this Chapter, but first it is necessary to examine democracy, its various interpretations, its relationship to liberalism and some philosophical presuppositions that support this political doctrine. Many apprehensions surrounding the theory of religious democracy are caused by conceptional ambiguities concerning the description of democracy and its possible models. We must define what it is that democracy means, whether or not there is a unique and commonly agreed interpretation of democracy and what exactly distinguishes a democratic government from a non-democratic one. Without answering such questions it will be impossible to come to an objective and accurate conclusion regarding the issue of religious democracy.

What is Democracy?

The term democracy is derived from the Greek words 'demos' (people) and 'kratia' (rule), so democracy literally means 'rule by the people'. In other words it is a political doctrine in which it is believed the people possess the capacity needed in order to govern and regulate society. This idea originally emerged towards the beginning of the fifth century B.C. in ancient Greece, primarily amongst the Athenians. The city-state of Athens referred to itself as a democracy (from 500 B.C to 330 B.C) because all citizens (excluding women, slaves and non-residents) could participate in political decisions. Abraham Lincoln's famous definition of 'Government for the people and by the people'[1] refers to this model of participatory democracy.

Throughout the long history of political thought, many different forms of democratic government have emerged and declined, they often came into being almost completely independently of one another, as Dahl writes:

> *It would be a mistake to assume that democracy was invented once and for all, as, for example, the steam engine was invented...democracy seems to have been invented more than once, and in more than one place. After all, if the conditions were favorable for the invention of democracy at one time and place, might not similar favorable conditions have existed elsewhere? I assume democracy can be independently*

---

[1] Daniel Webster in 1830 (thirty three years before Lincoln's definition) said: people's government, made for the people, made by the people and answerable to the people.
Cf: *Patterns of Democracy*, p. 1.

invented and reinvented whenever the appropriate conditions exist.[2]

Although the root meaning of the Greek term 'demokratia' is clear and straightforward (rule by the people), it is necessary to properly define what constitutes 'demos' (the people). Historically the criteria of who ought to be included in 'demos' to rule and participate in political decisions, as a citizen has been an ambiguous and contentious issue. In the most ancient models of democracy, 'the people' did not include all adults; women and slaves were not given the right to participate in the political system. And even today there are noticeable disagreements amongst modern interpretations of democracy about who should be included among the 'demos'. For example, even though the principle of equality was firmly established in the American declaration of independence in 1776, the right for free men to vote on an equal basis was not granted until 1850. Black males were prevented from voting until the fifteenth constitutional amendment some twenty years later. And females, both free and enslaved, were not given the right to vote until the nineteenth constitutional amendment in 1920.[3] Democracy in the above mentioned forms, is an imaginary and inapplicable idea in large scale societies.

In general, both advocates and critics agree that 'rule by the people' - in the truest meaning of the people – never existed and is never likely to exist. It is impossible for any democratic regime to be fully democratic, as it will always fall short of the criteria that emanates from its self-evident

---

[2] Robert Dahl, *On Democracy*, Yale University Press, 2000, p. 9.
[3] Sulaiman Sadek Jawad, *Democracy and Shura*, Published in Liberal Islam, p. 97.

meaning. The virtues and advantages that are mentioned to justify democratic government undoubtedly require 'participatory democracy', which delegates decisions to citizens, so, in a single meeting or during an election, people are able to express their opinions. That is why the Greeks passionately supported 'assembly democracy'. Obviously this system is inherently limited by practical considerations, in a small political unit such as a city, assembly democracy provides citizens with desirable opportunities for engaging in the process of governing themselves. This original conception of democracy, which was embodied in Greek city-states, is possibly the most appropriate to the true meaning of the term (excluding the fact that only a minority could vote). However modern democracies within nation-states exist on a much greater scale than before. Consequently, modern theories of democracy, despite their alleged efficiency when dealing with the problems of large-scale societies, effectively decrease the political participation of the people. In modern democratic theories 'the people' (demos) are replaced by 'representatives', so that a small proportion of the population are made responsible for looking after the affairs of the people, thus 'rule by the people' becomes 'rule by representatives elected by a majority of the people'.

A significant cause for the confusion concerning the meaning of 'democracy' at present is due to the fact that it has developed over several thousand years and ultimately stems from a variety of sources. Our understanding of the term 'democracy' is not necessarily the same as an Athenian's understanding of the term. Greek, Roman, Medieval and Renaissance notions have intermingled with those of later centuries to produce a mosaic of theories and practices that are often deeply inconsistent.[4]

If any attempt to apply the original meaning of democracy to the nation-state is impossibly absurd, and moreover if there is no commonly agreed definition of the democratic system amongst its advocates, it should be reasonable to concentrate on what at present are known as democratic states in order to recognize its major elements and what distinguishes them from a non-democratic state.

Even though, in theory, political philosophers and theorists have presented various models of democracy such as 'elitism', 'participatory', 'pluralistic' and 'corporate', in practice representative democracy is the prevailing norm among contemporary democratic systems. The major characteristics of modern democracy, according to Dahl are as follow:

Elected officials: control over government decisions concerning policy is constitutionally vested in officials elected by citizens. Thus, modern, large-scale democratic governments are representative.

Free, fair and frequent elections: elected officials are chosen in frequent and fairly conducted elections in which coercion is comparatively uncommon.

Freedom of expression: citizens have a right to express themselves on political matters without danger of severe punishment; this includes criticism of officials, the government, the regime, the socio-economic order and the prevailing ideology.

---

[4] *Democracy and its Critics*, p. 2.

Access to alternative sources of information: citizens have a right to seek out alternative and independent sources of information from other citizens, experts, newspapers, magazines, books, etc.

Associational autonomy: citizens have the right to form relatively independent associations or organizations, including independent political parties and interest groups in order to achieve their various rights.

Inclusive citizenship: No adult permanently residing in the country and subject to its laws can be denied the rights that are necessary for the five political institutions listed above.5

These help explain the political reality of democracy as a political system in which people participate, and as a method and process for making collective political decisions. The key point is that democracy requires 'majority rule', meaning that majority support should not only be necessary, but also sufficient for enacting laws. Some contemporary writers even go so far as to argue that majority rule is a definition, not a requirement of democracy.[6] Also numerous advocates of democracy do not confine the role of the people to the mere distribution of political power, or participation in the process of collective political decisions (via their representatives), rather, they have a right to control governors. Mayo writes:

> *In short, a political system is democratic to the extent that the decision makers are under effective popular control.[7]*

---

[5] *On Democracy*, pp. 85-86

[6] *Democracy and its Critics*, p.135.

[7] H.B. Mayo, *An Introduction to Democratic Theory*, Oxford University Press, 1960, p. 60.

In summary, democracy is a political system, which acknowledges the right of the people to participate in political decisions, either directly or indirectly through elected representatives, to distribute and regulate the political power under the rule of a majority. Political prerequisites such as free, fair and frequent elections, freedom of expression, inclusive citizenship and so on, are necessary in order to insure the soundness of the process.

Democracy and Liberalism

Most contemporary democracies are liberal democracies: a combination of the democratic political system, and the liberal political ideology, that places emphasis upon specific rights and values such as private possession, negative freedom, individualism and toleration. Therefore, liberal democracies embody two distinct features; the first of these is the liberal conception of a limited government; this is that the individual should enjoy a degree of protection from arbitrary action of government officials. This limitation of government - which is often referred to as the theory of limited democracy – is rooted in the belief that fundamental rights and values supported by liberalism possess a moral standing and philosophical grounds, that are altogether independent of democracy and the democratic process. These rights and values serve as a limitation or restriction on what can be enacted by means of the political system. Citizens are entitled to exercise certain rights and should not be threatened by the powers of state and governmental processes. Liberals believe in protecting these rights from infringement, even though they may be by democratic means.

This is why liberal attitudes towards democracy have historically been distinctly ambivalent. In the nineteenth century, liberals often perceived democracy as something threatening or dangerous. The central concern for liberals has always been that democracy could evolve to become the enemy of individual liberty and pluralism. The rule of the majority is the 'democratic solution' to conflicts that people have regarding their interests and opinions. This means that the will of the greatest number of people should prevail over that of the minority. In other words, democracy comes down to the rule of 51 percent, a prospect that Alexis de Tocqueville (1805-1859) famously described as 'the tyranny of the majority'. Individual liberty and minority rights can thus potentially be crushed in the name of the people.[8]

Liberals have expressed particular reservation concerning democracy, and have crafted a network of checks and balances in order to reconcile the advantages of democracy and fundamental liberal rights and values. This combination creates a model of democracy that, as Heywood says, has three central features:

> *First, liberal democracy is an indirect and representative form of democracy. Political office is gained through success in regular elections, conducted on the basis of formal political equality – 'one person, one vote; one vote, one value'. Second, it is based upon competition and electoral choice. This is ensured by political pluralism, a tolerance of a wide range of contending beliefs, conflicting social philosophies and rival political movements and*

---

[8] Andrew Heywood, *Political Ideologies*, Macmillan Press, 2nd Edition, 1998, p. 43.

parties. Third, liberal democracy is characterized by a clear distinction between the state and civil society. This is maintained both by internal and external checks on government power and the existence of autonomous groups and interests, and by the market or capitalist organization of economic life.[9]

As far as our discussion – the relationship between Islam and democracy – is concerned, it is fundamental to distinguish between democracy just as a method to form a political system or as a process for making collective decisions opposed and liberal democracy as one of the possible models of democracy consisting of an ideological framework of beliefs and values. Many opponents of religious democracy have failed to distinguish between democracy as a method and liberal democracy, which in principal represents a particular political philosophy and doctrines with its own beliefs regarding human nature, human rights, ends and moral values.

Benefits of Democracy

There are many advantages that make democracy more desirable than any other feasible alternative political system. Even though to attain all of the potential benefits is beyond the capacity of current democracies, these ideal consequences cannot be overlooked. When properly implemented and regulated, the democratic political system should in theory produce a series of beneficial objectives.

Avoiding tyranny: Democracy reduces the likelihood of a tyrannical or autocratic government obtaining power.

---

[9] *Ibid.*, p. 46.

However, this does not mean that democracy can totally guarantee the prevention of oppressive or dictatorial rule, or that it is entirely capable of preventing injustice in society. For example, the Nazi party in Germany (1933-1945) obtained power through the manipulation of the democratic and free-electoral systems. Advocates of democracy argue, though, that in the long-term a democratic process is less likely to do harm to the interests of the citizens than a non-democratic one.

Protecting essential rights: Democracy guarantees its citizens a number of fundamental rights that undemocratic systems do not grant. These political rights are all necessary elements of democratic political institutions.

Human development: It is claimed that democracy fosters human development more fully than any practical alternative. This claim is controversial and very difficult to substantiate. The only way to test this assertion is by measuring human development in democratic and non-democratic societies.

Political equality: Only a democratic government can guarantee a high degree of political equality amongst citizens.

Protecting essential personal interests: Democracy assists people in protecting their own fundamental interests. It allows people to shape their life in accordance with their own goals, preferences, values and beliefs.[10]

Perhaps the most common justification given for democracy is that it is essential for the protection of the general interests of the persons who are subject to a democratic state.

---

[10] *On Democracy*, pp. 45-57.

However, it is worth mentioning that this attempt to justify democracy has been attacked by some democratic theorists. For example, John Plamenatz argues that we cannot compare governments and, as a reasonable empirical judgment, conclude that "the policies of one have in general done more than those of the other to enable their subjects to maximize the satisfaction of their wants". This is particularly true if the governments are not of the same type and the values and beliefs of the people concerned differ greatly. Moreover people do not and should not prefer democracy to its alternatives because they believe it is better at maximizing the satisfaction of their desires. They should instead favor it because it provides people with certain rights and opportunities or reject it because it does not.[11]

Foundations of Democracy

It is widely believed that political theories have philosophical or metaphysical foundations that justify every political ethos or system amongst its alternatives. Referring to these foundations for the justification of political thought is considered important because they represent the basis from which the system has emanated. It is insufficient merely to examine publicly admitted elements and values that have emanated from this basis, as these have ultimately grown around a political doctrine and logically cannot prove the validity of that political theory. The prevalent approach maintains that the question of justification is also a question of truth. A valid and justified political system must be consistent with human nature, human common goods and ends and other related moral-philosophical truths. This method of political theorizing (also known as

---

[11] John Plamenatz, *Democracy and Illusion*, Longman, 1973, pp. 164-168.

foundationalism) is omnipresent in the history of political thought, especially so during the age of enlightenment, when thinkers such as John Locke and Emmanuel Kant presented rational foundations as basic elements of contemporary western political culture. Political foundationalism presupposes that there is a correct answer to every fundamental political question, and through the appropriate method of thinking, political truths are made available.

Recently, some advocates of liberal democracy, in contrast to traditional supporters of democratic governments, have inclined to justify their political system without reference to a particular interpretation of human nature or any comprehensive moral, religious or philosophical doctrine as a basis. John Rawls (1921-2002) and Richard Rorty, the contemporary American philosopher, are to prominent figures of this modern anti-foundationalism movement in political thought. They present a 'political' democratic liberalism instead of a 'philosophical' one. Their justification for this model of political thought is not rooted in any specific philosophical or moral doctrine. John Rawls writes:

> *Political liberalism, then, aims for a political conception of justice as a freestanding view. It offers no specific metaphysical or epistemological doctrine beyond what is implied by the political conception itself.[12]*

This attitude, its influence and its relevance to our main debate (Islam and democracy), will be assessed later in the

---

[12] John Rawls, *Political Liberalism*, Columbia University Press, 1996, p. 10.

Chapter. It is now necessary to briefly refer to some philosophical foundations mentioned by some thinkers to justify democracy as the most desirable political system.

Intrinsic Equality

The belief that all humanity is made intrinsically equal by man's own inherent nature and instincts is a concept supported by the great religions of Islam, Christianity and Judaism. For some, however, the idea of inherent equality provides a justification for democracy because it indicates that all human beings are of equal intrinsic worth and no person is naturally superior to another. Locke says:

> *Though I have said above...that all men by nature are equal, I cannot be supposed to understand all sorts of equality: age or virtue may give men a just precedence: excellency of parts and merit may place others above the common level...and yet all this consists with equality, which all men are in, in respect of jurisdiction or dominion over one another, which was the equality I there spoke of, as proper to the business in hand, being that equal right that every man hath, to his nature freedom, without being subjected to the will or authority of any other man.*[13]

The politically implicit meaning of the last sentence of this quotation is that the good or interests of each person must be given equal consideration, hence, people have a right to express their will and no one has the right to make a decision on behalf of them except with their permission. For

---

[13] John Locke, *Two Treatises of Government*, Peter Laslett (ed), Cambridge University Press, 1970, p. 322.

advocates of democracy who refer to the intrinsic equality, every guardianship model of government, which entrusts the authority to a few people (guardians) instead of people themselves, must therefore be incompatible with the idea of the intrinsic equality of people. Locke ascribed the intrinsic quality to 'men' instead of 'the people' because in his own era the theory that men alone qualify as 'active citizens' was common (As indicated earlier, it was not until the twentieth century that women gained the right to vote). It is also worth mentioning that Kant too firmly supported political freedom and according to his view, the legislative authority should be placed in the hands of a representative assembly, whose members are elected by a majority of voters in each district. However, Kant's franchise is restrictive. He assumes that it should extend only to adult males who own property and that these persons alone qualify as 'active citizens'. Others are merely 'passive citizens' and while they must be assured the same civil rights and legal equality as everyone else, they should not be allowed to vote.[14]

If we were to overlook this restriction and ascribe the intrinsic equality to all human beings (men and women), it could not justify democracy as the best desirable political system, as essentially there is no necessary connection between admitting intrinsic equality and the necessity of a democratic state. Robert Dahl states that intrinsic equality is quite compatible with guardianship as well. He writes:

> *As I have already said, nothing in the assumption of intrinsic equality implies that Able, Baker and Carr are the best judges of their own good or interests,*

---

[14] Allen Rosen, *Kant's Theory of Justice*, Cornell University Press, 1993, pp. 34-35.

suppose it were true that a few people like Eccles not only understood much better than the others what constitutes their individual and common good, and how best to bring it about, but could be fully trusted to do so. Then it would be perfectly consistent with the idea of intrinsic equality to conclude that these persons of superior knowledge and virtue, like Eccles, should rule over all the others. Even more: if the good of each person is entitled to equal consideration, and if a superior group of guardians could best ensure equal consideration, then it follows that guardianship would definitely be desirable and democracy just as definitely would be undesirable.[15]

Priority of the Will of the Majority over Rightness

A rare conception of democracy supposes that the democratic system and the rule of the majority can guarantee correct decisions and right answers to political needs. People who individually are the best judge for their private, personal affairs also are the best judge in public affairs (policy decisions). The political judgments of the majority reflect what is best and right for the community. According to this theory, there is no need for a few experts (guardians) with specific moral and scientific-philosophical knowledge to perform correct policy decisions, because the performance of the experts is no better than the people's choices. The choice of the majority would be based upon certainty and would achieve a correct result. However, the practical and realistic approach to democracy, supported by its advocates, does not accept that the rule of the majority is a guarantee for right decisions. It admits that people have a right to

---

[15] *Democracy and its Critics*, p. 88.

decide, however it also accepts that voters and their representatives may not always make the correct decisions. The validity of the democratic political system is not owed to the knowledge that the will of the people (majority) reflects the correct outcomes and true social good. The political legitimacy of democracy, instead, rests upon the will and consent of the people, not upon their reason or rightness. This means that although there is no rational-philosophical certainty that democratic political decisions are right, it is simply sufficient that these decisions are outcomes of the will of the people and their exercising of their practical rights and freedoms. Michael Walzer writes:

> *Democracy rests, as I have already suggested, on an argument concerning freedom and political obligation. Hence it is not only the case that the people have a procedural right to make the laws. On the democratic view, it is right that they make the laws – even if they make them wrongly.*[16]

Since the legitimacy of the democratic system rests on people's rights instead of their valid knowledge, there is no reason to suppose firstly that the power of the people must be limited by the rightness of what they decide, and secondly that a few experts ought to be empowered to review what the people do and step in when they move beyond those limits and make incorrect decisions. The presupposition of such a view is that there is a small group of people, in every society, that can recognize the truth better than society as a whole can, hence they must have a right to intervene. Democracy in principle absolutely disagrees with this

---

[16] Michael Walzer, "Philosophy and Democracy", in *Political Theory*, Volume 9, No 3, August 1981, p. 386.

procedure, for the people's rule does not rest upon their knowledge of truth. If we admit that finding objective knowledge, true answers, and right decisions is possible and philosophers are those who can be presumed to attain the truth, then the tension between philosophy and democracy is inevitable because the democratic system fails to reconcile between the rule of majority and the authority of truth (philosophy). Walzer says:

> *Nor can the philosophical instrument be a majority amongst the people, for majorities in any genuine democracy are temporary, shifting and unstable. Truth is one, but the people have many opinions, truth is eternal, but the people continually change their minds. Here in its simplest form is the tension between philosophy and democracy. The people's claim to rule does not rest upon their knowledge of truth...the claim is most persuasively put, it seems to me, not in terms of what the people know, but in terms of what they are. They are the subjects of the law, and if the law is to bind them as free men and women, they must also be its makers.*[17]

Many advocates of the democratic system as the best desirable political system strive to justify the detachment between democracy and the issue of truth by stating misgivings about the possibility of attaining objective knowledge about public good and moral truths. For instance, Robert Dahl emphasizes that not only is the justification for democracy independent of any specific answer to the epistemological ontological questions about the nature of moral judgments, but also democracies should have

---

[17] *Ibid.*, p. 383.

misgivings about such claims. For him, we are entitled, indeed obliged, to look with the greatest suspicion on any claim that another possesses objective knowledge of the good of the self that is definitely superior to the knowledge possessed by the self.[18]

General Freedom

Democracy, not only as an ideal, but in actual practice prerequires certain rights and liberties. A truly democratic government could only be established within a political culture that profoundly supports these rights and freedoms. That is why advocates of democracy always stress its relationship to freedom and view democracy as the best political system that maximizes and protects general freedoms such as freedom of opinion and expression and freedom of religion. Accordingly some liberties are preconditions for the emergence of a democratic state, whereas others (such as the freedom of self determination) are seen as results of such a state. Thus one can conclude that democracy is desirable because freedom in general and freedom of self-determination in particular is desirable. In other words, to govern oneself, to obey laws that one has chosen for oneself, and to be able to determine ones destiny is a desirable state of affairs. On the other hand, however, human beings cannot exist in isolation from society, and it is essential for them to live in association with others and to live in association with others naturally requires that they must sometimes obey collective decisions that are binding upon all members of the association. Democracy maximizes the potential for self-determination amongst society because its members still govern themselves. Dahl claims that this

---

[18] *Democracy and its Critics*, pp. 66, 101, 103.

justification for democracy has been endorsed by all those, from Locke onwards, who have believed that governments ought to be based upon the consent of the governed.[19]

In a similar manner, democracy is also justified by the assumption that this political system maximizes 'moral autonomy'. A morally autonomous person is one who defines his own moral principals. Dahl states a deeper reason for valuing self-determination; that the freedom to govern oneself is in fact an expression of the value of moral autonomy, but he neglects to discuss the arguments for why moral autonomy should be respected.[20]

Personal Autonomy

Dahl believes that the cornerstone of democratic beliefs is the presumption of personal autonomy, namely the assumption that no person is, in general, more likely than yourself to be a better judge of your own good and interests, or to act in order to bring them about. Consequently you should have the right to judge whether a policy is, or is not, in your best interest. On this assumption, then, no one else is more qualified than you to judge whether the results are in your interest.[21]

It is quite clear that this justification, if any, merely supports the assembly model of democracy, which is appropriate for a small-scale society in which people have an opportunity to share directly in the process of making political decisions, whereas most present day democracies are representative. In the representative model of democracy, the choice of people

---

[19] *Ibid.,* p. 89.
[20] *Ibid.,* p. 91.
[21] *Ibid.* p. 99.

about their goods and interests is confined to electing representatives. Dahl in his later book (On Democracy) refers to this dark side of representative democracy:

> *The dark side is this: under a representative government, citizens often delegate enormous discretionary authority over decisions of extraordinary importance. They delegate authority not only to their elected representatives, but, by an even more indirect and circuitous route, they delegate authority to administrators, bureaucrats, civil servants, judges and at a still further remove to international organizations...popular participation and control are not always robust, and the political and bureaucratic elites possess great discretion.*[22]

Even though the roots of democracy mentioned by advocates who believe in foundationalism are not restricted to what has been discussed above, these four principals are viewed as more significant than the others. In comparison with the second approach i.e. the political or pragmatic defense of the democratic state, which does not rest on any specific foundation or doctrine to justify this political system, foundationalism is significant because with a comparative discussion one can make judgment and recognize how compatible Islam and the foundations of democracy might be. Before further debate about these foundations, it would be appropriate to explore the modern approach to liberal democracy (anti-foundationalism). As indicated previously, John Rawls, one of the most influential political philosophers of the twenty century, in his latest works insists that we should present a political conception of liberal

---

[22] *On Democracy*, p. 113.

democracy – liberal justice – instead of the comprehensive conception that rests upon specific moral and philosophical doctrines. For him this new political liberalism is 'free standing' with no reference to any particular comprehensive doctrine or specific moral-philosophical foundation. He writes:

> *While we want a political conception to have a justification by reference to one or more comprehensive doctrines, it is neither presented as, nor derived from, such a doctrine applied to the basic structure of society...but as a distinguishing feature of a political conception is that it is presented as free standing and expounded apart from, or without reference to any such wider background.[23]*

By emphasis on a freestanding view of liberal democracy – a well ordered, just, democratic society, which does not rest on particular doctrines – he hopes that this conception can attain an overlapping consensus among reasonable comprehensive doctrines. The political conception of liberal democracy with its freestanding view supplies appropriate circumstances to be endorsed by citizens who belong to various comprehensive religious or philosophical doctrines. He says:

> *The problem, then, is how to frame a conception of justice for a constitutional regime such that those who support, or who might be brought to support that kind of regime might also endorse the political conception provided it did not conflict to sharply with their comprehensive views. This leads to the idea of a*

---

[23] *Political Liberalism*, p. 12.

> *political conception of justice as a freestanding view*
> *starting from the fundamental ideas of a democratic*
> *society and presupposing no particular wider*
> *doctrine, so that it can be supported by a reasonable*
> *and enduring, overlapping consensus.*[24]

Rawls' starting point is the ideas and values that are latent in the public political culture of contemporary western liberal democracies. His political conception of a well-ordered democratic society based on the principles of justice, is formed upon western culture without any attempt to justify these ideas and values. Rawls writes:

> *In order to state what I have called political*
> *liberalism, I have started with a number of familiar*
> *and basic ideas implicit in the public political culture*
> *of a democratic society. These have been worked up*
> *into a family of conceptions in terms of which political*
> *liberalism can be formulated on understood.*[25]

Richard Rorty, a famous American philosopher, maintains that Rawls does not attempt to justify democratic institutions through philosophical foundations. Rorty writes:

> *Rawls is not attempting a transcendental deduction of*
> *American liberalism or supplying philosophical*
> *foundations for democratic institutions, but simply*
> *trying to systematize the principals and intuitions*
> *typical of American liberals.*[26]

---

[24] *Ibid.*, p. 40.

[25] *Ibid.*, p. 43.

[26] Richard Rorty, "The Priority of Democracy to Philosophy", in *Reading Rorty*, Alan R. Malachowski (ed), Oxford: Basil Blackwell, 1990, p. 289.

For Rorty, the sources latent in the public political culture of liberal democracies seem to be all that is available, and so must be all that is required to justify the liberal democracy political system. Rorty says:

> *It is not evident that [liberal democratic institutions] are to be measured by anything more specific than the moral intuitions of the particular historical community that has created those institutions. The idea that moral and political controversies should always be 'brought back to first principals' is reasonable if it means merely that we should seek common ground in the hope of attaining agreement. But it is misleading if it is taken as the claim that some particular interlocutor has already discerned that order.[27]*

For many thinkers it is obvious, that this method of justifying a political system, which consists of merely invoking the basic elements of a public political culture, because these cultural elements and values grow and thrive around that political system, cannot logically support this argument. This anti-foundationalist approach to the contemporary democratic system comes to the conclusion that advocates of liberal democracies are free to ignore critics whose criticisms question the moral intuitions of western liberal democracies. Rorty, in principle, disagrees with any attempt to provide rational foundations for systems of values and concepts.[28]

---

[27] *Ibid.*, p. 290.
[28] Stephen Mulhall and Adam Swift, *Liberals and communitarians*, Blackwell, 2nd Edition, 1996, pp. 259-261.

Obviously this form of justifying a democratic state does not provide an opportunity for comparative critical discussion between Islam and democracy. This anti-foundationalist approach as a first step and starting point wants us to completely admit all basic values of western liberal democratic culture while allowing no room for criticism or philosophical discussion concerning these values and foundations. As Rorty states "Rawls puts the democratic politics first and philosophy second."[29]

Limited Democracy versus Pure Democracy

Pure democracy or unlimited democracy is a political system in which all political questions are settled directly, without any restrictions, by the majority vote of citizens. Early liberals were concerned about pure democracy for its potential harms, for instance Kant maintained that pure democracy that relies upon the majority vote in an assembly, without any constitutional restrictions, subjects the individual to the whims of the masses, as it contains no constitutional safeguards against the tyranny of the majority and, therefore, it cannot protect personal rights. Justice demands that a people be given the right to make its own laws, but the right must be constrained by constitutionally guaranteed civil liberties. In Kant's view, political freedom embodied in voting and democratic processes, alone does not ensure civil freedom. The majority may fail to respect the rights of the minority.[30]

Conversely the idea of a limited democracy is based on the doctrine that there are many fundamental rights – including

---

[29] *Reading Rorty*, p. 291.
[30] *Kant's Theory of Justice*, p. 34.

political rights – that possess a moral standing and a philosophical ontological basis that is independent of democracy and the democratic process. Since the validity and foundational justification of these rights does not depend on majority rule or the democratic process, they can serve as limits on what can be done by means of the democratic process. Citizens are entitled to exercise these rights, against the democratic process if need be, to preserve fundamental political rights and liberties and in order to protect themselves from infringement even by means of the democratic process itself.[31]

The above-mentioned justification for limited democracy should not be restricted to fundamental rights; rather, it also embraces moral and religious values. According to this justification, whatever possesses a moral or philosophical standing – a reliable and valid foundation – independent of democracy and the democratic process, should be protected from possible democratic harms. Consequently the limits of democracy could be constitutional, moral or even religious. Theoretically, the limits of this type of democracy depend on what is crucial and most fundamental for citizens who choose democracy as their desirable political system.

For example, in the United States, since 1803 the Supreme Court, consisting of nine judges, has been assigned to declare whether legislation is 'constitutional' or not. Indeed they have the authority to review what the people and the people's representatives enact via the democratic process. Of course, the constitutional role of the Supreme Court judges extends no further than the enforcement of a written constitution that is itself based on democratic consent and is

---

[31] *Democracy and its Critics*, p. 169.

subject to amendments through the democratic process. The tension between judicial review and democracy occurs within the framework of the constitution. Even when the judges act in ways that go beyond upholding the textual integrity of the constitution, they generally claim no special understanding of truth and rightness but refer instead to historical precedents, long-established legal principals or common values. Nevertheless, the place they hold and the power they wield make it possible for them to impose philosophical constraints on democratic choice.[32]

Having referred to these primary points concerning democracy, it is now time to address the central purpose of this Chapter; that is the possibility of a religious (Islamic) democracy.

What is the Conception of a 'Religious Democracy'?

It goes without saying that 'pure democracy', which delegates all dimensions of public affairs including legislation to majority rule without limitation, is absolutely incompatible with Islam. Essentially every school of thought, ideology and religion that follows a set of beliefs, values or rules independent of the will and desire of people cannot approve unlimited democracy. These values and rules must be protected and this cannot be insured by the will of the majority, as majorities in any form of democracy are shifting and unstable. Even political ideologies such as Liberalism and Socialism are in need of a constitution to control a purely democratic process and to protect their fundamental values and beliefs from possible harm from

---

[32] Walzer, "Philosophy and Democracy", in *Political Theory*, Volume 9, No. 3, August 1981,pp. 387-388.

majority rule. On the other hand, democracy and the democratic process do not provide us with a comprehensive ideology, way of life or any substantial values. Democracy is but a method among other alternative methods for overcoming difficulties in decision making in an association or society. The philosophical foundations mentioned to justify the democratic system, fail to uphold it as a reliable means to attain truth and righteous decisions. Majority rule is too weak to be presented as an alternative to comprehensive religious, moral and philosophical doctrines. In fact what gave democracy superiority over other alternative systems is far removed from any philosophical or ideological basis; instead the democratic system is made desirable in comparison to other political systems because of its practicality.

Democracy as a method does not contain fixed, unalterable or absolute moral and philosophical ideas and values. However, in order for a political regime to be democratic, it must meet some criteria. A democratic political system should provide the opportunity for the people to participate, at least in some significant political decisions, to express their ideas, orientations and needs, to distribute political power through free elections and be able to regulate and bring to account the governors. These political rights and duties of the people in a democratic regime could be dealt with within a fixed framework consisting of specific rights and values. In current limited democracies these frameworks are embodied in constitutions, and constitutions in turn are influenced by values and beliefs that people of each country respect and support. Muslim advocates of democracy cannot accept 'pure democracy' as Abu al-Ala Mawdudi says:

> *Islam is not democracy: for democracy is the name given to that particular form of government in which sovereignty ultimately rests with the people, in which legislation depends both in its form and content on the force and direction of public opinion and laws are modified and altered, to correspond to changes in that opinion.*[33]

Therefore the key issue concerning religious democracy is whether Islam has the capacity to draw an appropriate framework for a democratic government that meets the above-mentioned criteria. As I have indicated in the earlier pages of this Chapter, many Islamic thinkers believe that Islam has delegated significant political as well as social roles and duties to Muslims. In Islam, no conflict exists between the supreme authority of religion – the definite and unquestionable status of divine laws and Islamic values – and the political status of people in an ideal Islamic state. As there are limitations for the will and desire of the people, they have authority within the framework of Islamic rules and values. Hence, a majority of the people or their representatives have no power to legislate or make judgments that contradict Islam. At the same time the governors in an Islamic state must respect the rights, will, and authority of the people. Ayatollah Khomeini, the founder of the Islamic Republic of Iran during a meeting with the representative of Pope VI said:

> *I do not want to impose (my will) on my people, and Islam does not permit us to establish a dictatorship. We follow our nation's votes and act according to*

---

[33] Abu al-A'la Mawdudi, *Political Theory of Islam*, Karachi: Maktaba-e Islami, p. 30.

their views. We have no right, God has not conferred such a right to us, and the Prophet (pbuh) never permitted us to impose our ideas upon Muslims.[34]

Smoothing the Path to Religious Democracy

The advocates of Islamic democracy usually refer to the shura (consultation) as the most important Islamic teaching that supports and justifies the authority of people in an Islamic government. Rashid al-Ghannouchi (Tunisia, born 1941) writes:

The Islamic government is one in which:
1- Supreme legislative authority is for the shari'a, which is the revealed law of Islam, which transcends all laws. Within this context, it is responsibility of scholars to deduce detailed laws and regulations to be used as guidelines by judges. The head of the Islamic state is the leader of the executive body entrusted with the responsibility of implementing such laws and regulations. ·
2- Political power belongs to the community (ummah), which should adopt a form of 'shura' which is a system of mandatory consultation.[35]

Thinkers like Sadek Sulaiman (Oman, born 1933) maintain that shura in Islam includes basic elements of democracy. He says:

---

[34] Ruhollah Khomeini, *Sahifa Nur,* Tehran: Ministry of Islamic Guidance, Volume 10, p. 181.
[35] Rachid Ghannouchi, "Participation in Non-Islamic Government", in *Liberal Islam*, p. 91.

As a concept and as a principle, shura in Islam does not differ from democracy. Both shura and democracy arise from the central consideration that collective deliberation is more likely to lead to a fair and sound result for the social good than individual preference.[36]

The Holy Qur'an explicitly proposes and encourages that public affairs and the governance of the ummah should be based upon shura:

' And those who respond to their Lord and keep up prayer, and their rule is to take counsel amongst themselves. [Chapter 42, Verse 38]

And ask pardon for them, and take counsel with them in the affair. [Chapter 3, Verse 159]

The second verse orders the Prophet (pbuh), who receives revelation and enjoys infallible knowledge, to take counsel with believers in management of public affairs. This command shows the fundamental significance of the participation of Muslims in social and political affairs. It is somewhat an exaggeration to suppose that the shura is the functional equivalent of western parliamentary democracy because there are some controversies amongst scholars about the political status of shura. For instance, those who believe in the theory of Caliphate, emphasize that members of the council only have a duty to express their opinion with no right to make political decisions. Accordingly if the Caliph refers to the assembly to take their opinion regarding rulings,

---

[36] *Liberal Islam*, p. 98.

which he wants to adopt, their opinion is not binding on him, even if it is a consensus of majority opinion.

What makes shura one of the basic elements of Islamic democracy, it seems, is the fact that shura refers to one of the significant essentials of democracy. Democracy in its long history has had evolutions and alterations, but matters such as public participation, the rule of law and the responsibility and accountability of governors can be recognized as essential to democracy. In conclusion, the assumption that the Islamic political system could be a democratic one, merely implies that Islamic teachings endorse and agree with the essentials of democracy. From this point of view, there is no doubt that the verses of the Holy Qur'an concerning shura along with some transmissions from the prophet and Imams emphasize on the necessity of public participation in political and social affairs. But the question concerning the political role of consultation (shura) in the process of making decisions still remains. Is consultation merely a religious duty of the ruler of the Islamic state, or is he bound by the decisions of those consulted?

The last verse [159] of Surah al-Imran [3] verifies the view that shura is not binding upon the ruler, for the Almighty God delegates the final decision, after consultation, to the Prophet (pbuh):

And take counsel with them in the affair, so when you have decided then place your trust in Allah. [Chapter 3, Verse 159]

However, the practice of the Holy Prophet, according to some traditions, testifies that he had implemented and respected the opinion of the believers even when it was against his own views. It is recorded that the Prophet not only consulted with his experienced or close companions, but sometimes he held open meetings in which all Muslims were invited. The consultation that took place about the battle of Badr and Uhud was one such example. In the case of Uhud he gave precedent to the opinion of the majority of Muslims over his own concerning the location of the battlefield and decided to fight outside the city of Madina. He also consulted the people concerning the treatment of prisoners of war following the battles of Badr and al-Khandaq.[37]

Clearly, however, the Prophet did not consult the Muslims concerning religious affairs or divine matters. His consultations were restricted to war, peace and ordinary public affairs that were not determined by revelation and were not amongst the situations in which divine order determined must be done. For example, with regard to the treaty of al-Hudaybiyah the Prophet (pbuh) did not submit to the opinion of the majority of his companions who were in disagreement with the covenant, it was not in fact a consultation but a series of complaints made to the messenger regarding the terms of the peace. He rejected their suggestions to break his promises and continued to respect the agreement, which he had made because it was a command of Allah (swt). He told them: "Verily I am the servant of Allah and his messenger. I shall never disobey his order."

---

[37] Ibn Kathir, *Umda,* Volume 3, p. 63; Ibn Hisham, *Sireh Ibn Hisham*, Volume 2, pp. 272-273.

In short, even though the shura in its historical function within the Islamic world does not totally overlap with the modern concept of democracy and the political status of parliament in contemporary representative democracies, it would be appropriate for shaping a limited democratic model for an Islamic state. The Qur'anic emphasis on the status of shura as an essential aspect of the Islamic political system – according to those who interpret the word for amr in both of the two verses relating to shura, as referring to governmental affairs – makes way for defining a determined systematic role for the people's representatives (members of the shura) within the body of the Islamic state. The above-mentioned verses are silent about how the form and mechanism of shura in an Islamic political system might be, consequently the constitutional approach inclines to determine and stabilize the political status of shura (people's authority) under the supreme authority of Islam does not confront any religious problem.

The second element, however, often mentioned by advocates of religious democracy as an appropriate approach to an Islamic democratic state is bay'ah. In the first Chapter, the meaning of 'bay'ah' has already been discussed. Here, the aim is to examine its legal nature, for it is supposed that its political function is the same as the function of an election in democratic systems. It should be noted that bay'ah in the sense of adherence to a religion (as occurred between the Prophet and his supporters from Madina before Hijrah) or recognition of a pre-established authority by other means (such as the testamentary designation, such as the bay'ah of people to the second caliph Umar) is irrelevant to our debate. Bay'ah as a means and method of designating a person as a ruler (caliph) among other legitimate methods is held to be the same as democratic election in its legal nature. This political view exclusively belongs to Sunni jurists, because Shia political thought, except that of the Zaydis, maintains that the Imamah is acquired by election within the Alid family. The bay'ah has never been able to play this role, for the Shia recognize only one method of designating the Imam. He is appointed through the testament (nass) of one in the legitimate line of descent.[38]

This sense of bay'ah is a supposed contractual agreement between those who elect and he who has been designated as the ruler. As far as democracy is concerned, for at least two reasons, bay'ah is not simply and solely a democratic election. Firstly, bay'ah implies binding obedience to the ruler, and since it is a contractual agreement, like commercial agreements such as bao (to sell), the obedience of the elected ruler as a religious duty, would be obligatory. Secondly, this obligatory obedience is life long, whereas the democratic process of appointing a person as ruler is merely temporal with no religious implications.

One of the most important characteristics of a democratic government is its accountability to its people. A democratic state must be accountable and its citizens must have the right to criticize its policies and functions. Advocates of religious democracy maintain that al-amr bi'l-maruf wal nahy'an al-munkar (enjoining good and forbidding evil) is one of the most significant Islamic duties placed upon Muslims and it should render the Islamic state accountable. Many Qur'anic verses emphasize on this fundamental injunction, which if Muslims take seriously would produce a healthy and healthy

---

[38] *Encyclopedia of Islam*, Volume 1, p. 1113a.

society that is far removed from tyranny, injustice and dictatorship. Almighty God says in the Holy Qur'an:

> *And from amongst you there should be a party who invite to good and enjoin what is right and forbid the wrong, and these it is that shall be successful.* [Chapter 3, Verse 104]

> *And (as for) the believing men and believing women, they are guardians of each other, they enjoin good and forbid evil.* [Chapter 9, Verse 71]

It is an Islamic duty, incumbent upon all Muslims, to concern themselves with the health and well being of society, to oppose injustice and immorality, and to scrutinize the actions of those who undertake governmental affairs. There exists a mutual responsibility between the rulers and those whom they rule to implement and uphold the Islamic shari'a and this provides a clear framework and basis upon which citizens may question the actions and policies of their governors with regards to their socio-religious duties. As the most-noble Messenger (pbuh) in a famous tradition says:

> *Every one of you is a shepherd (of the community), and all are responsible for their dependants and herd.*[39]

In order to fulfill this obligation (to monitor governmental functions) there is a requirement for certain conditions to be met, such as the freedom of speech and to criticize as well as access to accurate and objective information. Otherwise, the

---

[39] *Sahih Muslim*, Hadith 1829.

active participation of people in public-religious duties such as providing constructive feedback and criticisms toward the governors and standing for justice and truth would be impossible. It is obvious that Islam does not concur with individual freedom to the extent prevalent in western culture. However, the preconditions of an Islamic and democratic government that respects the rights of the people and their contribution in socio-political affairs, are outlined by the Qur'an and Sunnah (valid traditions). For example the Qur'an encourages believers to listen to different opinions and to select the best of them:

> *Therefore give good news to my servant. Those who listen to the word, then follow the best of it; those are whom Allah has guided, and those it is who are men of understanding.* [Chapter 39, Verses 17-18]

There are many narrations in historical and religious texts documenting dialogue and debate that occurred between Shia Imams and non-Muslim intellectuals in which disbelievers (even atheists) were able to express their ideological views so long as they were voiced as academic opinions and kept within the circles of scholarly debate, rather than attempting to propagate them. In a true Islamic state, it is the right granted to the people that they be kept aware of affairs in society and government.

Imam Ali (pbuh) once explained the mutual rights and duties that exist between an Imam (leader) and the people:

> *It is your right that I must not hide any secret, except that of war, from you. And that I should not take over*

*matters (without your consultation or awareness)
other than those concerning divine laws (hukm).[40]*

Aside from the obvious distinction between religious democracy and western liberal democracy, the former holds the same essential advantages as any democratic government. These include the participation of citizens, the distribution of political power by election, political accountability of governors, constitutionalism and political transparency as well as mutual responsibility between the rulers and the ruled. Religious democracy however, is far more desirable for Muslims than any feasible alternative because of the supreme role of the shari'a in providing a basis for, and shaping the growth of, the contents of this political system. It is also desired because of the qualities and moral-religious commitments that the governor must have as the leader of Muslim society.

For instance, constitutionalism and accountability in secular, western democracies as Nathan Brown says, has expressed itself most frequently in human authored constitutional texts and rights, whereas religious constitutionalism is defined under the authority of the shari'a. Therefore, the religious government is not only accountable with regard to people's rights and needs, but also with regard to the shari'a and divine laws. He writes:

Many Muslims have come to believe that the crisis of political accountability can be solved by insisting that Muslim governments rule within the bounds fixed by the Islamic shari'a. In essence, this demand renders the Islamic shari'a as a kind of constitution.

---

[40] Ibn Abi al-Hadid, *Sharh-e- Nahjul Balaqeh*, Volume 16, p. 17.

> *Governments may not cross the boundaries firmly*
> *established by the Islamic shari'a; rulers are held*
> *accountable to God's law.*[41]

In summary, although governments throughout history have often ignored the political teachings of Islam, the main purpose here is to show that these significant teachings smooth the path towards the establishment of a religious democracy.

Religious Democracy and its Critics

As indicated earlier, adversaries of religious democracy are scattered amongst both fundamentalists and liberal advocates of a secular state. All of them arrive at the conclusion, through various perspectives, that any composition between Islam (the authority of religion) and democracy (the authority or consent of the people) is an incompatible thesis. Here, the major arguments that the major critics of religious democracy have presented will be assessed.

Religious Democracy is Paradoxical

Critics of religious democracy maintain that there is an inherent antagonism between the fundamental aspects of the Islamic creed and the basis of democracy. According to this view, those who subscribe to the idea of religious democracy ignore the true nature of religion and overlook the epistemological foundations of democracy. The democratic system is based upon pluralism that places emphasis upon

---

[41] Nathan Brown, "Islamic Constitutionalism in Theory and Practice", in *Democracy the Rule of Law and Islam*, Eugene Cotran (ed), Kluwer Law International, 1999, p. 491.

freedom instead of regulation, diversity as opposed to homogeneity, and multiplicity rather than unity. According to pluralistic doctrine, no single person, group or school of thought can possess or claim to possess the absolute truth or that it's understanding and opinions are correct and that all others are false. Truths are distributed amongst humanity, hence, every opinion is but a composition of truth and falsehood, and consequently no opinion has superiority over another, and cannot claim such. People are free to follow and support any opinion they decide upon, whether it be religious or secular, theistic or atheistic, moral or immoral. The unlimited freedom of choice is one of the most important foundations of democracy, a foundation that Islam is opposed to. Hamid Paydar writes:

One of the epistemological foundations of democracy is the obscurity of truth and its distribution amongst all human beings, however, if an ideology or religion should call itself the sample of truth, maintaining that other religions and opinions are manifestations of infidelity, polytheism and misleading, it would not be compatible with democratic government. Islam, according to some verses of the Qur'an introduces itself as a unique right and true religion. Verses such as "This then is Allah, your true lord; and what is there after the truth but error" [10:32] "And whoever desires a religion other than Islam, it should not be accepted from him" [3:85] and the opening verses of Surah Taubah (repentance) are in contradiction to man's freedom of choice. [42]

---

[42] Hamid Paydar, "The Paradox of Islam and Democracy", in *Modara wa Modiriyat*, Abdul Karim Surush (ed), Tehran: Serat Publication, 1997, pp. 525-526.

This view emphasizes on the inflexibility of Islamic laws and the absolute authority of the shari'a as evidence of incompatibility between Islam and democracy. Obviously the interpretation of democracy stated above does not represent what exists in an ordinary democratic state. It is a particular version of democracy mixed with extreme liberalism, which asserts the absolute neutrality of a liberal democratic state. For this new approach a desirable political system should ignore any conception of good and should not based upon any particular philosophical-religious doctrine of life. As Galston says:

> *According to this view, the liberal state is desirable not because it promotes a specific way of life but precisely because it alone does not do so. The liberal state is 'neutra' amongst different ways of life. It presides benignly over them, intervening only to adjudicate conflict, to prevent any particular way of life tyrannizing over others, and to ensure that all adhere to the principals that constitute society's basic structure.*[43]

It is not our objective to discuss whether the neutrality of a political system is possible. However, the fact is that no form of political life can be justified without appealing to certain ideas and values concerning society and the individual. Some advocates of liberalism maintain that liberal theorists covertly employ theories concerning goodness. However, their adamant denial of any reference to

---

[43] William .A Galston, *Liberal Purposes*, Cambridge University Press, 1991, p. 80.

a basis or foundation reduces the strength of their argument and leaves their theories vulnerable to criticism.[44]

Regardless of whether a neutral government is feasible or not, there is no doubt that Islam is in complete disagreement with many underlying values of liberal democracy, including secularism, pluralism and radical individualism. Consequently the above-mentioned theory merely explains the general incompatibility of Islam with liberalism and specifically the new conception of a 'liberal state'. This, nevertheless, does not in any way undermine other versions of limited democracy, including religious democracy.

Usurpation of God's Sovereignty

Some Muslim thinkers who emphasize on Islamic governance argue that democracy is contradictory to Islamic principals because it involves the legislation of laws, and there are may verses of Qur'an that demonstrate that legislation is reserved for Allah (swt).

> *Indeed judgment (hukm) is only for Allah.* [Chapter 6, Verse 57]

> *And in whatever thing you disagree, the judgment thereof is with Allah.* [Chapter 42, Verse 10]

> *And if you were in dispute in anything amongst yourselves, refer to Allah and His Messenger.* [Chapter 4, Verse 59]

---

[44] *Ibid.*, p. 79.

In conclusion, Islam holds that sovereignty is with God (Divine law = shari'a) and not with the ummah (people), thus the ummah does not possess the right to legislate on any matter. For example, even if all the Muslims were to gather together and agree to permit usury, usury would remain prohibited because it is a decree from Allah and Muslims have no choice in the matter. On the other hand, in democracy sovereignty is with the people, thus they are able to legislate according to their own free will and desires, either directly or indirectly via the representatives they have elected.[45]

The Egyptian revivalist scholar, Sayyid Qutb holds that the essential doctrine of liberal democracy, namely the sovereignty of man, is a usurpation of God's sovereignty and a rebellion against His authority, for it subordinates the individual to the will of other individuals instead of God's governance on the earth.[46] Clearly this approach to religious government, in principal, should not ignore the administrative and executive role of the people in an Islamic state, because for them the problem of legislation is fundamental. This approach insists that the believers cannot frame any law for themselves, nor do they have the right to alter or modify God's laws. This assumption has emanated from the idea that it is incumbent upon Muslims to follow shari'a and to restrict all actions and principals to this basis. It is not allowed for them to undertake or leave anything except after understanding the rule of Allah regarding it. Furthermore, those who deny any legislative role for the

---

[45] Abdul Qadeem Zalloom, *Democracy is a System of Kufr*, London: Al-Khilafah Publication, p. 35-37.

[46] "Sayyid Qutb, Ideologue of Islamic Revival", in *Voices of Resurgent Islam*, John Esposito (ed), Oxford University Press, 1983.

people maintain that the Islamic shari'a contains rules for all past events, current problems, all possible incidents and that it encompasses the actions of man completely and comprehensively. Allah says:

And we have sent down to you the book as an exposition of everything, a guidance, a mercy and glad tidings to those who have submitted themselves to Allah. [Chapter 16, Verse 89]

Accordingly, Muslims are allowed to make use of the sciences and thoughts of human beings unless they contradict Islam. However, with regard to laws and legislation it is prohibited for Muslims to devise and obey un-Islamic rules because it is impossible to find a human action that does not have an evidence or a sign that indicates its rule in the Quran. This is due to the general meaning of His saying 'exposition of everything'.[47]

Since the above view is both influential and popular amongst Islamic revivalist movements, it would be both convenient and useful to examine its various aspects. In order to do this, one must first clarify the meaning of "God's sovereignty", then the assumption that all legislative authority rests with God and that believers and qualified jurists (fuqaha) cannot frame any laws for Muslim society should be examined. It should also be emphasized that there is a lack of knowledge concerning the Islamic model of democracy, which insists on the sovereignty of God as well as people's authority in limited aspects of political affairs. The followers of this doctrine focus solely on a comparison between their

---

[47] *Democracy is a System of Kufr*, pp. 22-25.

conception of an Islamic state and a purely democratic (or liberal democratic) model.

By definition, sovereignty is the claim of ultimate political authority, subject to no higher power with regards to the legislation and enforcement of political decisions. In the international system, sovereignty is the claim by the state to independent self-government and the mutual recognition of claims to sovereignty is the basis of international society.[48]

Through regarding sovereignty as the basis and foundation of the political power that a government relies upon in order to be able to exercise its power and organize its domestic and international relationships, the idea that sovereignty as a political term has no connection to God has come to being. Therefore those who attribute the quality to God confuse between the religious status of God amongst believers and the political power of a state referred to by the term 'sovereignty'. Hence many thinkers such as Fazlur-Rahman essentially deny any attempt to translate the supremacy of Allah into political sovereignty.

> The term 'sovereignty' as a political term is of a
> relatively recent coining and denotes definite and
> defined factors in a society to which rightfully belongs
> coercive force in order to obtain obedience to its will.
> It is absolutely obvious that God is not sovereign in
> this sense and that only people can be and are
> sovereign, since only to them belongs ultimate

---

[48] *Oxford Concise Dictionary of Politics*, p. 464.

coercive force i.e. Only their 'word is law' in the politically ultimate sense.[49]

As a matter of fact, every formed state has sovereignty regardless of how its political hegemony and power are established and shaped. So, all political models of government - democratic, dictatorship, guardianship and even a military government established by a coup d'etat - so long as it remains in power and can exercise ultimate political authority, possesses sovereignty. In the Islamic ideology, however, there is no unique origin for the establishment of political sovereignty and thus the fundamentally crucial question in this regard is one of 'legitimacy'. Which form of political sovereignty is the legitimate one? Amongst political philosophers there are several answers to this significant question. The idea that 'only people can be and are sovereign', as Fazl ur-Rahman stated, represents the democratic approach to this question. Certainly, for philosophers who believe in 'guardianship' such as Plato, the rule of majority and the consent of the people does not legitimize the political sovereignty of a government.

Therefore, sovereignty as such could be created through a number of means and in different forms, but every political doctrine presents its own specific interpretation of legitimate sovereignty and emphasizes on one factor as an essential element of a legitimate state. In the view of those who support the doctrine of an Islamic state, the legitimacy of a government is strongly tied to the extent of that government's commitment to the shari'a as well as Islamic

---

[49] Fazlur-Rahman, "The Islamic Concept of State" in *Islam in Transition*, Ponohue and John Esposito (eds), Oxford University Press, 1982, p. 269.

teachings and values. Muslim thinkers construe the phenomena as God's sovereignty because God's will is embodied in his legislations and His will and orders have priority over the will and orders expressed by the rulers of an Islamic government, who are obligated to rule in accordance with divine laws (shari'a).

With regards to this interpretation of God's sovereignty with its particular insistence on his supremacy in legislation, the key issue that arises is whether sovereignty prevents the believers from any form of legislation. This important question distinguishes between religious democracy and the above-mentioned doctrine that does not recognize any right for the believers to frame any law for themselves. Religious democracy, as emphasized before, is based firmly upon the belief in the ultimate authority of almighty God, including his legislative sovereignty. But it is essential to recognize that the unquestionable legislative superiority over dimensions of Muslim's life is one issue, and their frequent need for appropriate, fresh and temporal laws to handle new and unusual situations is another. Muslims society, like all other societies, is in need of new laws and regulations in order to adapt its legal system with the frequent alterations in social relationships, namely, new developments in human lifestyle, technological development and cultural–economical changes. Social change in its broad meaning regularly produces many fresh judicial questions, which often cannot be resolved without new legislation.

The conception that Islam is perfect, comprehensive and all-embracing with regards to the needs of human beings, particularly the judicial-legislative necessities that arise, and that the Islamic legal system consequently includes all rules required for a desirable Islamic way of life, with no need to draft new legislation and laws, can be interpreted in two ways. The first notion incorporates a misinterpretation of the idea that Islam is indeed a perfect religion. This theory asserts that in every case in which mankind is in need of laws, there are appropriate rules that already exist in the shari'a that can be automatically applied. Islam contains every law that people require in order to handle their private and public affairs. In conclusion, there remains no legal vacuum to justify the existence of another legislative sovereignty to derive new laws. According to this view, Qur'anic verses such as "And we have sent down to you the book as an exposition of every thing" [16:89] should be interpreted as supporting this view, because the word 'everything' embraces all rules we need in the various dimensions of our life, at all times and in every model of social formation. Regarding the Islamic legal system, all judicial demands would be satisfied either by in advance prepared rules or through Ijtihad (fuqaha derive new laws by referring to Islamic sources), which in turn is not legislation. Through ijtihad the faqih recourse to the sources of shari'a to declare the position of Islam with regards to new questions and situations, this in its nature is completely separate from legislation. Islamic jurists have no right to legislate, they merely are able to understand and announce to believers what Almighty God has declared.

Small-scale societies have a relatively simple social structure that can be easily regulated by a basic set of rules. However, contemporary society is considerably larger and possesses a vast social structure permeated by many complex interrelationships. In such an environment, every circumstance and aspect of public life requires a flexible legal network, consisting of both fixed and changeable rules, in order to be able to stay in harmony with the demands of a growing and modern society. The existence of ahistorical, non-temporal and fixed laws is a significant characteristic that is common in many comprehensive legal systems, especially in the Islamic legal code, nevertheless, the importance of temporal, changeable rules that every government must legislate according to new economic, social and political situations cannot be ignored. These policies are required to protect the interests of society and to overcome different social difficulties concerning education, taxation, security, exports, immigration and so on. Therefore the adoption of policy is one of the most important functions of a government.

The shari'a is perfect, not because we do not need any kind of legislation or because all the rules needed have been previously prepared, rather it is because Islam is the most perfect of all legal systems. It consists of comprehensive and all-inclusive divine laws and Islamic jurisprudence also has specific elements, which render it a dynamic and flexible system that is capable of operating hand-in-hand with changes in society and reality. One of the most significant aspects of this structure is the right of a well-qualified jurist (Wali al-faqih mujtahid a-adil) to issue rulings and commands. If the shari'a has already providing a verdict regarding a specific issue, it is an obligation upon the Islamic state to adopt the ruling of the shari'a. If a situation arises in which the shari'a is ambiguous or there exists a difference of opinion concerning the divine law, the opinion and edict of the Wali Amr (who carries the responsibility of rulership in the absence of the infallible Imam) has precedence over all others. In the case where there exists no obligation or prohibition in the shari'a, it is permissible for the just faqih to issue a governmental order necessitated by the interest of Islam and Muslims. Since the just faqih has legitimate authority (wilayah) and legislative sovereignty other governors, including those elected by the people such as members of parliament and the president, should be appointed by the just faqih otherwise they would have no legitimate authority to make governmental rules and decisions. For instance Ayatollah Khomeini says:

In the absence of the guardianship of a faqih or divine ruler, the taghut (illegitimate authority) will prevail. If the president is not appointed by a just faqih, he would be illegitimate.[50]

In letters appointing the members of the Islamic Revolutionary Council in Iran as well as the first premier, referring to the above points, he writes:

As a person who enjoys the wilayah of the sacred religion, I appoint him...any opposition to this government is tantamount to opposition of shari'a.[51]

Therefore, being elected by the majority or obtaining public consensus does not automatically grant legislative sovereignty or legitimate religious authority to rule and govern Islamic society. And in cases that governors have been appointed by the just faqih – even elected officials – their authority for making decisions and orders cannot contradict the shari'a. Finally, in instances where there is no

---

[50] *Sahifa Nur*, Volume 9, p. 253.
[51] *Sahifa Nur*, Volume 5, p. 31.

clear indication from the shari'a because the case is totally new, and without previous record, it is the responsibility of the fuqhaha (jurists) to deduce the appropriate rule from Islamic sources.

The legitimate status of the majority is what truly distinguishes religious democracy from all other conceptions of the democratic state, for religious democracy limits the authority of the people in accordance with the legislative sovereignty of God. Whereas in non-religious democratic states, the sovereignty of elected individuals is not restricted by shari'a, and the doctrine explicitly assumes democracy as a secular system detached from the authority and sovereignty of God. It thus fails to make a fair assessment of the religious model of democracy and the relationship between Islam and democracy.

The Problem of Legal Equality

Legal equality is often highlighted as one of the crucial foundations of democratic government. Consequently, every political theory that wishes to categorize itself as democratic must respect the legal equality of its citizens. Some critics of religious democracy maintain that Islam is not compatible with democracy on the grounds of some inequalities endorsed within the Islamic legal system.

Islam may be credited with having disseminated the spirit of equality and brotherhood amongst its followers, nevertheless the inferior status of three groups, namely non-Muslim citizens, slaves, and women, and their inequality before the law as

> *compared with free male Muslim citizens do not help*
> *in smoothing the path to a democratic system.*[52]

Even though the modern conception of democracy emphasizes on all embracing legal equality, democracy in its nature – as the history of political thought – testifies that it is compatible with legal inequalities. As discussed before, in ancient models of democracy only free male landowners had the right to participate in the process of making decisions for city-states. In modern democracies, the right for all free men to vote on an equal basis was not granted until 1850. Males of African origin were denied the right to vote until 1870, and females, both those who were free and the slaves, were not granted the right until the 19th constitutional amendment in 1920. Moreover, even the modern conception of democracy does not rest upon a complete, unexceptional, and all-inclusive legal equality. Instead it relies upon the principal that all adult members of society are considered equal in political rights, and are able to participate in voting and the distribution of political power. Therefore the existence of non-political legal inequalities, in principal, is not incompatible with democracy. Suppose that according to a legal system, women have not been granted the right to become a judge or religious leader, or that they inherit less than males, obviously these non-political inequalities do not undermine the idea of establishing a democratic system.

No one can make a credible attack against the Islamic ideology because of its supposed endorsement of slavery, slavery was an age-old, and universally accepted institution, which was only officially abolished in the western world less

---

[52] Forough Jahanbakhsh, *Islam, Democracy and Religious Modernism in Iran*, Brill, 2001, p. 49.

than two centuries ago when the anti-slavery movements emerged around the world. However, when Islam was revealed, slavery was considered a completely natural aspect of human culture as well as an inseparable element of society. Islam moderated this institution and encouraged believers to emancipate their slaves. In fact, the concept of freeing slaves is an important element in the Islamic system of punishment. The acceptance of slavery by Islam should not, therefore, be considered an obstacle for democracy. In summary, there is no doubt that there are some differences in shari'a between Muslims and non-Muslims (for example in retribution), between men and women (for example in inheritance), but these legal inequalities have no connection to political equality and citizenship. For example, in the constitution of Iran as a model of Islamic democratic government, many articles emphasize the equal rights of citizens, men and women, Muslim and non-Muslim:

All people of Iran, whatever their ethnic group or tribe to which they belong, enjoy equal rights; color, race, language and the like, do not bestow any privilege. [Article 19]

All citizens of the country, both men and women, equally enjoy the protection of the law and enjoy all human, political, economic, social and cultural rights, in conformity with Islamic criteria. [Article 20]

Reconciling Islam and Liberal Democracy

Muslim advocates of religious democracy strongly support the conception of a democratic political system possessing a religious framework drawn by shari'a. In other words, a judicial (fiqhi) based model of democracy that respects the authority of the people regarding God's sovereignty and Islamic law. They emphasize upon the accountability of the government, the participation of the people in political affairs and the implementation of the shari'a. According to their conception of religious democracy, the political power belongs to the people, but their authority is limited by the shari'a. Hence, it is not in the people's power to make political decisions that contradict Islamic rules and values. The basic structure of a fiqhi based society, namely the system of rights and duties, should be defined according to instructions and limitations set forth by Islamic teachings in general and shari'a in particular.

Some Muslim intellectuals attempt to present a model of Islamic democratic government, which in principle welcomes with open arms many underlying values of contemporary liberal democracies. As a notable sample of this modernist approach there is the conception of Abdul-Kareem Soroush (an Iranian intellectual born in 1945) regarding religious democracy. Here we will briefly explore a political approach that strives to reconcile Islam and the western conception of human rights, justice and rationality, by reducing the status of shari'a to juridical conflicts with no connection to the management of society or the regulation of social relationships. The basic elements of this doctrine are as follows:

i   In contrast to the prevailing conception of a religious society and Islamic government, that is essentially fiqh based and defines a religious society as one wherein the implementation of shari'a is the ultimate aim and major function of the religious state, the above mentioned doctrine does not give Islamic jurisprudence such a crucial role. According to a fiqh-based interpretation of religious society and Islamic governance, the rights and responsibilities of people have been defined and determined by Islamic laws, in other words the issue of human rights is defined within a religious context, particularly jurisprudential arguments. However, the above doctrine insists that defining human rights, and thus human duties, belongs to the extra-religious area and should be determined outside the domain of religion and shari'a.

ii   "The first issue concerning human rights is that it is not a solely legal (fiqhi) inter religious argument. Discussion of human rights belongs to the domain of philosophical theology and philosophy in general. Furthermore, it is an extra-religious area of discourse. Like other debates on matters that are prior to religious understanding and acceptance such as the existence of God, and the election of the Prophets, human rights lies outside of the domain of religious"[53]

iii   Religious law (shari'a) is not synonymous with the entirely of religion; nor is the debate over the democratic religious government a purely jurisprudential argument, so we shouldn't define the religious society according to the extent of its adoption of shari'a. The prophets founded a society based on faith and spirituality, not on legality. The heart of a religious society is freely chosen faith, not coercion and conformity. Religious society is based upon free, invisible faith, and dynamic and varied religious understanding.[54]

---

[53] Abdul Karim Soroush, *Reason, Freedom and Democracy in Islam*, Mahmoud Sadri and Ahmad Sadri (trs), Oxford University Press, 2000, p. 128.

[54] *Ibid.*, pp. 134-141.

iv   The jurisprudential governing and attempt to resolve social and public difficulties by Islamic laws must be replaced by rationality and scientific magnanimity. Islamic jurisprudence (fiqh) was a solution for simple, underdeveloped societies that had simple, uncomplicated relationships. Fiqh could handle and successfully organize such societies, but the problems of complicated modern societies would be resolved solely by rationality and science instead of jurisprudence.[55]

v   Democratic religious regimes need not wash their hands of religiosity nor turn their backs on God's approval. In order to remain religious, they, of course, need to establish religion as the guide and arbiter of their problems and conflicts. But, in order to remain democratic, they need dynamically to absorb an adjudicative understanding of religion in accordance with the dictates of collective reason. Furthermore, every democratic religious government must be mindful of both the inside and the outside of the religion in order to remain faithful to both of its foundations.[56]

vi   Debates concerning justice, human rights and the methods of government cannot be resolved through intra-religious debate: these are extra-religious arguments that deeply influence the understanding and practice of religion. Religious understanding must constantly renew and correct itself according to philosophical-theological debate concerning human rights, the meaning and nature of justice, the effective method of government and so on. The legal and

---

[55] Abdul Karim Soroush, *Qesseye Arbab-e Marefat*, Tehran: Serat Publication, 1995, pp. 54-55.

[56] *Reason, Freedom and Democracy in Islam*, pp. 128-129.

jurisprudential schools of thought should harmonize their achievements with these novel insights.[57]

Having accepted these premises, one comes to the conclusion that many substantial changes of modern humankind in its ideas, attitudes, worldviews and lifestyle must be admitted and respected by religion. These profound and widespread alterations include the desirable political system, human rights, the structure of fundamental rights and duties and the limited role of religion in human life. According to this doctrine, these significant changes should be noticed as new realities and truths, hence, religious knowledge must try to acknowledge and adopt itself to these facts. Therefore Muslims should not strive to deduce their political system from Islamic sources or form their social relationships according to the shari'a, instead they have to shape the fundamental basics of their society (i.e. The system of rights and duties) to become consistent modern mankind's world views, ideas and perspectives. The keystone of this political approach consists of the concept that the traditional Islamic thought – religious knowledge – is temporally limited and must therefore undergo a drastic metamorphosis in order that it be brought into line according to the views of "modern mankind".

This political doctrine suffers from three major categories of weakness. The first of these is that the fundamental aspects of this theory, presupposed by a specific doctrine about the nature of religious knowledge, rests on a subjective approach to the interpretation of texts. This subjective approach, called by Soroush "theoretic evolution and devolution of

---

[57] *Ibid.*, p. 148.

shari'a", insists that religious knowledge and the science of religion are relative to presuppositions, and in addition, that they are also temporal. He states that since these presuppositions are varied and restricted by time, religious knowledge and the interpretation of religion is entirely human and this worldly. All of this implies that religion is constantly surrounded by a host of contemporaneous data and deliberations, thus the interpretation remains constant so long as these external elements are also constant. However, once they change, the change will be reflected in the understanding of religion as well. Consequently, religious texts (such as the Holy Qur'an and Islamic traditions or ahadith) do not carry their meaning on their own shoulders, instead it is necessary to situate them within a context. The interpretation of the text is in flux, and presuppositions are actively at work here. Therefore, the interpretation of religious texts is subject to expansion and contradiction according to the assumptions preceding them. These assumptions are part of the world's view of an age, which need not and usually does not enter the mind through any formal education or conscious adoption, but rather are utilized inadvertently and fluently.[58]

This approach to religious knowledge and the interpretation of texts has been strongly influenced by subjectivist schools of interpretation particularly the German philosopher Georg Gadamer (died 2001) and the philosophical hermeneutics of his famous book "Truth and Method" (First German edition 1960).[59] According to these, the horizon of the reader (his

---

[58] Abdul Karim Soroush, "The Evolution and Devolution of Religious Knowledge," in *Liberal Islam*, pp. 245-246.

[59] I have written a few books and articles concerning the exploration and criticism of this hermeneutical approach for instance refer to:

presuppositions, attitudes and expectations) share in the process of interpretation, thereby making the reader more than a passive observer who merely receives the message of the text, rather he is an active participant who creates the meaning of a text, or at least the horizon of the reader shares in the process of constructing a meaning around the text. Hence, according to this theory, admitting modern and popularly viewed and shared ideas as extra-religious presuppositions is acceptable, even if this should interfere in the interpretation of religion. Examples of such ideas include the western conception of human rights, political system and the social formation of rights and duties. Below are a few brief criticisms of this conception of the nature of religious knowledge and understanding religious texts.

i   When referring to a religious text, the fundamental aim of interpretation for believers and religious scholars is to understand the 'intention' of the author (for instance the intention of God in divine revelation and what the Prophet had in mind with regard to interpretation of his hadith). To achieve this understanding, they seek objective and valid interpretations of the texts. Obviously every form of interference originates from the reader's prejudices, presuppositions and expectations, which imposing a specific meaning upon the text, this is obviously harmful for any attempt to interpret religious texts.

ii   It is quite possible to subjectively interpret a religious text with no regard to the intentions of its author or its context. This form of interpretation is known as tafsir bi rai

---

"The Hermeneutical Reflection of Heidegger," in *Transcendental Philosophy*, Volume 3, No. 3, September 2002.
An Introduction to Hermeneutics (Persian), Tehran, 2001, Chapters3&4.
The Alteration of Understanding Religion (Persian), Tehran, 1996.

(interpretation by personal attitude and prejudice), and is criticized in many traditions originating from the Prophet and the Imams (peace be upon them). Developing a meaning according to the varied presuppositions and prejudices that exist in human society, is not a question of feasibility, rather it is a question of legitimacy.

iii The assumption that religious texts do not carry their own meaning ignores the profound semantical relationship between words and meanings that is established in every natural language. This doctrine supposes that sentences of a text are empty vessels that a reader may place his own meaning within, as Soroush says:

Statements are hungry of meanings instead of being pregnant of them.[60] (meaning a statement requires a meaning to be given to it, rather than providing a meaning from it).

Clearly anyone who wants to use or understand a language must respect its structure and limitations. Why aren't we free to apply and understand an English text as we wish? The point is that the pre-established connection between words (and their meanings) in this language prevent us from doing so and these limit the shape and framework of our linguistic activity. Therefore, statements in a text are not devoid of meaning, rather they contain their own meaning and play a crucial role in the process of understanding and transmitting the intention of their author, although this is not to say that other elements (such as the context of the text) are not important.

---

[60] Qabs wa Bast-e theory e Shari'a, Tehran, Serat Publication, 1995, 3rd Edition, p. 287.

iv   This method of understanding in general, and understanding religious texts in particular, lends itself towards 'relativism'. It emphasizes that religious knowledge and the interpretation of text is a theory-laden, as Soroush writes:

> *Religious knowledge will be in continuous flux, and since it is only through those presuppositions that one can hear the voice of revelation. Hence the religion itself is silent.*[61]

This absolute relativism doesn't allow any room for the question of validity in interpretation of the text and religious knowledge. According to this approach, the validity of religious knowledge is connected to the validity of extra-religious knowledge, which consists of the presuppositions of each age, which in turn are varied and changeable. Whereas appealing to religious beliefs and knowledge based on reliability and validity of religious knowledge is undermined by this theory.

v   As a matter of fact readers face a text through their horizons that means they cannot ignore their knowledge, mental abilities, backgrounds and personal experiences concerning the context and content of the text. In other words, it is quite impossible that someone can overlook his own horizon and keep his mind empty when confronting a text, because our knowledge, experiences and so on are inseparable parts of our identity. This reality would not excuse free and nonstandard interference of the reader 's horizon in the process of the interpretation of the text. Indeed, the horizon of every reader consists of several

---

[61] Liberal Islam, p. 245.

categories and some of them play a crucial role in understanding the text. For instance, those who know Arabic and have suitable background in Islamic philosophy understand philosophical texts that have been written by Muslim philosophers in Arabic language much better than others. On the other hand, there are some elements whose influence we have to control during the interpretation of text, such as our prejudices and expectations that tend to impose particular and prejudged meanings over the text. That is why even some great advocates of philosophical hermeneutics notice the danger of some pre-understandings that hold back the correct process of interpretation. Heidegger and Gadamer emphasize that we have to distinguish between 'correct and incorrect', 'legitimate and illegitimate' conceptions and prejudices that come into understanding.[62] Consequently we are not free to allow our prejudgments, attitudes and fore conceptions to be presented in the event of understanding. Substantial changes in ideas, lifestyle and attitudes among modern humankind should not decide the message of a religion. Certainly these radical alterations sometimes create challenges and conflicts between a religion and modernism that require solutions, but reinterpretation of religion in favour of these new ideas and attitudes is not an appropriate solution, especially when we know that there is no justification for many of these modern concepts and approaches. Values such as consumerism, individualism, the liberal concept of freedom, secularism, free market (capitalism) and technology that make the major paradigms of

---

[62] Martin Heidegger, *Being and Time*, John Maquarrie and Edward Robinson (trs), Oxford: Blackwell, 1962, p.195; Hans Georg Gadamer, *Truth and Method*, London: Sheet& Ward, 1999, p. 298.

contemporary civilization and modern humankind 's lifestyle, have established themselves because of the personal preferences of the majority. However, most of these paradigms suffer from the problem of justification. Therefore, there is no reason for believers to blindly apply all modern values and conception to their religious texts and to reproduce their religious knowledge in accordance to them.

Another criticism of the above mentioned political doctrine concerns the ambiguous role of religion in this version of "religious" democratic government. The scope of political-social affairs concerns the practical aspect of Islam, which is largely embodied in Islamic law. Yet, this doctrine essentially denies the fiqhi based model of governing and, therefore, it remains ambivalent about the role (if any) of the shari'a with regards to the organization of social relationships and the process of making significant social-political decisions. On the other hand, if we endorse the claim that religious understanding should constantly be renewed and corrected in light of extra-religious presuppositions and that Islamic jurisprudential thought must harmonize its achievements with these novel insights obtained by human sciences, then what reason would justify and obligate us to harmonize our political-social decisions with such dependent, relative and changeable religious knowledge? Why shouldn't we just directly trust these novel extra-religious sights and presuppositions and relinquish religion?

Soroush emphasizes that religious democracies in order to remain religious, need to establish religion as the guide and arbiter of their problems and conflicts.[63] However, by overlooking the role of the shari'a in resolving the problems of contemporary modern societies, he does not explicitly state the mechanism upon which Islam might be the guide and arbiter of conflicts in the modern world.

Also significant is the fact that this doctrine fails to demonstrate why the problem of human rights and the system of rights and duties are extra-religious and why we shouldn't respect the explanation of religious sciences from intra-religious contents. It seems that the only reason that could possibly justify this approach rests on an extremely subjective conception of the nature of religious knowledge and the interpretation of texts, which has been criticized previously. In spite of this, there is no justification for ignorance concerning Islamic teachings, conceptions and laws with regards to human rights and duties. In cases where extra-religious notions and values contrast some Islamic teachings first of all we have to assess their capacity for truth-valid objective reasons that support and justify them. Clearly many fundamental notions in the modern conception of human rights are deeply influenced by concepts and values of liberalism, which in turn suffer from absence of valid justification. For instance the liberal conception of freedom plays a very significant role in shaping modern conceptions of human rights, while advocates of Liberalism still have not presented a valid convincing rational argument for this conception of liberty.

---

[63] *Reason, Freedom and Democracy in Islam*, p. 128.

Consider John Stuart Mill who tried to base and defend this freedom entirely on the principle of utility,[64] which as many critics have pointed out is ill-equipped to bear the burden. If personal liberty is as valuable as Mill insists, liberals should at least attempt to find a more permanent foundation for it than the disputable proposition - the principle of utility. Classical liberals like Mill are not the only liberals whose defense of individual freedom have run into trouble. Recent defenders of the liberal conception of personal freedom such as Friedrich Hayek and Isaiah Berlin do not present a convincing rational justificatory basis for it. Hayek stakes his defense of personal liberty on skepticism about moral rationality, while Berlin resorts to a kindred species of moral relativism. For Hayek 'reason' is powerless to determine 'ends' and, therefore, cannot tell us what we ought to do. Human intellect cannot by itself settle questions concerning value, especially questions about moral values. Consequently people personally must be absolutely free to choose.[65] Berlin, on the other hand, emphasizes on 'relativity of values' and the subjective nature of values to conclude that there is no objective higher good than the arbitrary or relative good each individual sets for herself.[66] The weaknesses of these arguments seem plain. How is it possible to claim that there are no objective values and that all values are purely subjective, and yet simultaneously state that we should always hold personal liberty in such high regard as to make it one of the central pillars of human rights and political life. If they are right that there are no objective

---

[64] John Stuart Mill, *On Liberty*, Edited by Gertrude Himmglfarb, Penguin Books, 1984, p. 69-70.

[65] Friedrich Hayek, *Law Legislation and Liberty*, University of Chicago, 1973, pp. 32-34.

[66] Isaiah Berlin, *Four Essays on Liberty*, Oxford University Press, 1969, pp. li, lvi, 172.

ends or values, then there can be no rational or objective grounds for valuating individual ends or liberty. In short, liberals must avoid the temptation to base their argument on relativistic or skeptical premises because it undercuts rather than supports their own arguments.

There are other points about the above mentioned political doctrine regarding the role of Islamic law (fiqh) in an Islamic government, which were discussed in the first chapter and do not need to be repeated again.

Final Word

During these four chapters I have attempted to explain the main elements of Imami Shi'a political doctrine and, where necessary, reconstruct some arguments that provide the reader an opportunity for better understanding the various dimensions of this political theory. However, it should be noted that there are still many things that must be discussed. Surely this political theory like any other theory is based on some philosophical foundations that have not been examined here in detail. One of these foundations, for instance, is the theory of self or the concept of human nature that underlies this political ideology. Obviously, each political ideology presupposes a specific concept of human nature because it tries to offer a desirable form of social-political life and naturally each form of life carries with it its own picture of human nature. As Hollis says:

> *All political and social theorists, I venture to claim, depend on some model of man in explaining what moves people and accounts for institutions. Such models are sometimes hidden but never absent. There*

is no more central or pervasive topic in the study of politics.[67]

The other significant moral-philosophical discussion pertains to the relationship between right and good and which one has priority over the other. Liberalism insists on rights and maintains that no definition of good life, human's ends and virtues, or ideal way of life can impose limits on individuals and what they select as their path in life. Therefore, liberalism instead of basing a conception of politics upon a specific concept of human nature and good life, concerns itself with rules that secure human rights, particularly rules that secure each individual the greatest amount of freedom to follow his own interpretation of what is good. Accordingly, political action including legislation, decision making, policy making and other governmental functions must be done independent of any concept of good and moral philosophy. Indeed neutrality and moral pluralism is a central value of modern Liberalism.

Joseph Raz writes:

Liberalism is committed to moral pluralism, that is to the view that there are many worthwhile and valuable relationships, commitments and plans of life which are mutually incompatible.[68]

Explicitly, Shi'a political thought contrasts the doctrine of Liberalism basing itself on underlying moral values drawn by Islamic jurisprudence and ethics. As a result, human

---

[67] Martin Hollis, *Models of Man*, Cambridge University Press, 1977.
[68] Joseph Raz, *Liberalism Autonomy and the Politics of Neutral Concern*, Midwest Studies in Philosophy, 1982, p. 7.

rights and duties must be defined according to these
fundamental Islamic rules and values instead of being
neutral. There is no doubt that a comprehensive assessment
of Shi'a political doctrine requires a profound comparative
discussion about these moral philosophical issues that are
absent in the present book.

The content of the book is concerned mostly with the
clarification of what is the desirable political regime among
Imami jurists. This type of discussion belongs to Islamic
political jurisprudence (al-fiqh al-siyasi), but it is correct to
keep in mind the fact that al-fiqh al-siyasi does not confine
itself to the question of 'what is the desirable model of state-
political regime- among Muslim thinkers?' The mutual
rights of the governed and governors, the method of
controlling political power at the various levels, and the
rights of minorities are just some significant examples of
political fiqhi debates that should be considered in an
exhaustive assessment of Shi'a political thought. In any case
it is hoped that this book has succeeded in explaining some
of the major elements of current Imami political theory.

Bibliography

1   Abd al-Raziq, Ali. 1925, *Islam wa Usul al-Hukm*, Cairo.

2   Al-Helali, Solaim ibn Qais. *Kitab al-Solaim*, Tehran: Dar al-Kotob al-Islamiya.

3   Al-Mufid (Muhammad ibn Muhammad ibn al-Num'an). 1972, *Al-Ershad*, Tehran.

4   Al-Senhoury, Ahmed Abd al-Razig. 1993, *Fiqh ul-Khilafah wa Tataworeha*, Cairo, 2nd Edition.

5   Al-Tusi, Muhammad ibn Hassan. 1958, *Al-Mabsut fi Fiqh al-Imamiya*, Tehran.

6   Al-Tusi, Muhammad ibn Hassan. 1411 AH, *Kitab al-Qayba*, Qom.

7   Amareh, Muhammad. 1986, *Al-Elmaniya wa Nehzatona*, Cairo; Dar al-Shorugh.

8   Berlin, Isaiah. 1969, *Four Essays on Liberty*, Oxford University Press.

9   Black, Antony. 2001, *The History of Islamic Political Thought*, Edinburgh University Press.

10 Borujerdi, Hussain. 1367 AH, Al-Badr Al-Zaher fi Salat ul-Jom'a wa al-Mosafer, Qom.

11 Brown, Nathan. 1999, "Islamic Constitutionalism in Theory and Practice" in *Democracy the Rule of Law and Islam*, Eugene Cotran (ed), Kluwer Law International.

12 Dahl, Robert. 1989, *Democracy and its Critics*, Yale University Press.

13 Dahl, Robert. 2000, *On Democracy*, Yale University Press.

14 Esposito, John. 1982, *Islam in Transition*, Oxford University Press.

15 Gadamer, Hans Georg. 1999, *Truth and Method*, London: Sheet & Ward.

16 Galston, William A. 1991, *Liberal Purposes*, Cambridge University Press.

17 Haery Yazdi, Mehdi. 1995, *Hekmat wa Hokumat*, London: Shadi Publication.

18 Haeri, Seyed Kazim. 1415 AH, *Wilayat al-Amr fi Asr al-Qayba*, Qom: Majma al-Fikr al-Islami.

19 Harrani, Ibn Shobeh. 1404 AH, *Tohaf al-Uqul*, Volume 1, Qom.

20 Hayek, Friedrich. 1973, *Law Legislation and Liberty*, University of Chicago.

21 Heidegger, Martin. 1962, *Being and Time*, John Maquarrie and Edward Robinson (trs), Oxford: Blackwell.

22 Heywood, Andrew. 1977, *Political Ideologies*, Macmillan Press.

23 Hollis, Martin. 1998, *Models of Man*, Cambridge University Press, 2nd Edition.

24 Hor al-A'meli, Muhammad Hassan. 1412 AH, *Wasael al-Shi'a*, Qom: Ahl ul-Bait Institution.

25 Jahanbakhsh, Forough. 2001, Islam Democracy and Religious Modernism in Iran, Brill.

26 Javadi Amoli, Abdul-llah. 1378 AH, *Wilayat ul-Faqih*, Qom: Esra Publication.

27 Khomeini, Ruhollah. 1981, *Islam and Revolution*, Hamid Algar (tr), Berkeley: Mizan Press.

28 Khomeini, Ruhollah. *Sahifa Nur*, Tehran: Ministry of Islamic Guidance.

29 Kurzman, Charles. 1998, *Liberal Islam* (a source book), Oxford University Press.

30 Leaman, Oliver. 1999, A Brief Introduction to Islamic Philosophy, Polity Press.

31 Lewis, Bernard. 1988, *The Political Language of Islam*, The University of Chicago Press.

32 Locke, John. 1970, *Two Treatises of Government*, Peter Laslett (ed), Cambridge University Press.

33 Maclean, Iain. 1996, *Oxford Concise Dictionary of Politics*, Oxford University Press.

34 Majlesi, Muhammad Baqer. 1985, *Behar al-Anvar* (110 Volumes), Tehran.

35 Mawdudi, Abu al-A'la. *Political Theory of Islam*, Karachi: Maktaba-e Islami.

36 Mayo, H. B. 1960, *An Introduction to Democratic Theory*, Oxford University Press.

37 Mill, John Stuart. 1984, *On Liberty*, Gertrude Himmglfarb (ed), Penguin Books.

38 Mohaqqiq al-Karaki. 1409 AH, *Al-Rasayel*, Muhammad al-Hassun (ed), The First Collection (Al-Ressala fi al-Salat ul-Jom'a), Qom.

39 Mulhall, Stephen and Adam Swift, 1996, *Liberals and Communitarians*, Blackwell, 2nd Edition.

40 Plamenatz, John. 1973, *Democracy and Illusion*, Longman.

41 Plant, Rymond. 1991, *Modern Political Thought*, Blackwell.

42 Plato, 1974, *Plato's Republic*, G. M. A. Grube (tr), Indianapolis.

43 Rawls, John. 1996, *Political Liberalism*, Columbia University Press.

44 Raz, Joseph. 1982, Liberalism Autonomy and the Politics of Neutral Concern, Midwest Studies in Philosophy.

45 Rosen, Allen. 1993, *Kant's Theory of Justice*, Cornell University Press.

46 Rorty, Richard. 1990, "The Priority of Democracy to Philosophy" in *Reading Rorty*, Alan R. Malachowski (ed), Oxford: Basil Blackwell.

47 Sachedina, Abdulaziz. 1988, *The Just Ruler*, Oxford University Press.

48 Sayyid Qutb, "Ideologue of Islamic Revival" in *Voices of Resurgent Islam*, John Esposito (ed), Oxford University Press.

49 Shahrestany, Abd al-Karim. 1956, *Al-Melal wal-Nehal*, Volume 1, Cairo.

50 Sharafud-Din, Abdul Husayn. *Al-Muraja'at*, Yasin T. al-Jibouri (tr), World Ahlul Bayt Islamic League (WABIL).

51 Shaikh al-Saduq (Muhammad ibn Ali ibn Babwayh), *Ellal al-Shariah*, Qom: Maktiba Davari.

52 Shaikh al-Saduq, 1405 AH, *Ikmal al-Din*, Ali Akbar al-Qafari (ed), Qom.

53 Shaikh Muhammad Hassan, 1398 AH, *Jawahir al-Kalam*, Tehran: Dar al-Kotob al-Islamiya.

54 Shaikh Hur al-A'meli, Muhammad ibn Hassan. 1412 AH *Wasael al-Shi'a*, Qom: Ahl ul-Bait Institute.

55 Soroush, Abdul Karim. 2000, *Reason, Freedom and Democracy in Islam,* Mahmoud Sadri and Ahmad Sadri (trs), Oxford University Press.

56 Soroush, Abdul Karim. 1995, *Qesseye Arbab-e Marefat*, Tehran: Serat Publication.

57 Taylor, Charles. 1997, "What's Wrong with Negative Liberty?" in *Contemporary Political Philosophy*, Robert E. Goodin (ed), Blackwell.

58 Watt, Montgomery. 1968, *Islamic Political Thought*, Edinburgh University Press.

59 Zalloom, Abdul Qadeem. *Democracy is a System of Kufr*, London: Al-Khilafah Publication.